Walks A1
Haunted London

John Wittich

S.B. Publications

First published in 1996 by S.B. Publications
c/o 19 Grove Road, Seaford, East Sussex BN25 1TP

ISBN 1 85770 091 0

Typeset, printed and bound by MFP Design & Print, Longford Trading Estate, Thomas Street, Stretford, Manchester M32 0JT; tel 0161–864 4540; fax 0161–866 9866.

Contents

Photographs:

Front cover: *Traitors' Gate, Tower of London*

Back cover: *St. Andrew's Terrace*

Title page: *Tyburn Tree site, Edgware Road*

Foreword

On several occasions in the past, I have voiced the opinion that there is more than one way of trying to find a solution to alleged reports of paranormal phenomena.

Either exhaustive tests may be carried out to try to establish, in a scientific and impartial way, the possibility as to whether certain strange tappings might be attributed to 'rats in the wainscot', or whether in fact a lately departed soul is really trying to announce its return to the surrounding in which its unfortunate demise took place.

It is easy for those of a romantic disposition, and who are addicted to stories of Gothic horror and mystery, to become totally absorbed in the apparently inexplicable phenomena which are said to sometimes manifest themselves, but there is even more satisfaction to be obtained if these manifestations can be found to establish between the present day and our mystical and historical past, a link of which they themselves could be a faint echo.

In London, where nearly every ancient building has its own story to tell, and almost every stone may be said to exude its own enigmatic auras of mystery, often combined with horror and tragedy, the researcher is given every opportunity to envelop himself in these age-old traditions by simply walking around such ancient piles as the infamous Tower of London, where the curtains of vapour gestated by the nearby Thames, can often be drawn aside for a brief few moments, to reveal some of the ancient secrets that lie therein.

In order to enjoy London to the full, especially when time is all too short, everyone should be furnished with a map or guide to reduce time wastage to the minimum. Unfortunately, the popular A–Z Guide does not include the local hauntings, and, in order to rectify this omission, John Wittich's useful book, *Walks around Haunted London,* comes to our rescue admirably, and every well-intentioned Ghosthunter should certainly carry a copy of it in his knapsack.

We wish this book well, because, with so many memories of our history being vandalised in the name of 'development', we could be very quickly arriving at the state when the only relics of our glorious and historic past are our 'spiritual' ones.

Tom Perrott,
Chairman of The Ghost Club
(founded 1862)

Preface

Whether, or not, one believes in ghosts, psychic phenomena occur in many buildings throughout London.

A small child entered a church and suddenly turned to her mother and said "Mummy, it's cold in here. Please let us go outside." The church was fully heated at the time! The child had felt a presence that could not be seen.

Other, older, visitors have reacted in much the same way and felt this presence in this City of London church.

Sceptics over the years have questioned the existence of ghosts. Many have put their doubts to the test and stayed the night in haunted rooms. Most have lived to tell their stories: some have been found dead in the morning. Others have been driven mad by what they saw or heard during their vigil. However, not all ghosts appear at night. Some brave the daylight to haunt their favourite places.

In writing this book I have consulted many books which record appearances of ghosts — human and inhuman. I can see no reason to suppose that ghosts have to take human form in their manifestations. Some appearances may take the form of an animal or bird, while it is not unknown for inanimate objects such as trees and stones to take on a ghostly aura. So called haunted trees and stones have been known to emit noises on windless nights and to be associated with the paranormal. Ghosts do not appear "to order", nor regularly, and only to those people who believe in them, and have the "second sight".

"I know they are there. I do not have the gift to see them"

— AN ANGLICAN PRIEST

In a newspaper interview in 1984 the then Bishop of Salisbury, The Rt. Reverend John Austen Baker, declared that he believed in ghosts and that he once saw one. He added that Christians should not be ashamed to look at explorations of the spiritual order by either religious or scientific methods.

"Happy Ghost Hunt"

The Author,
Hallowe'en 1995

Chiswick — by the river

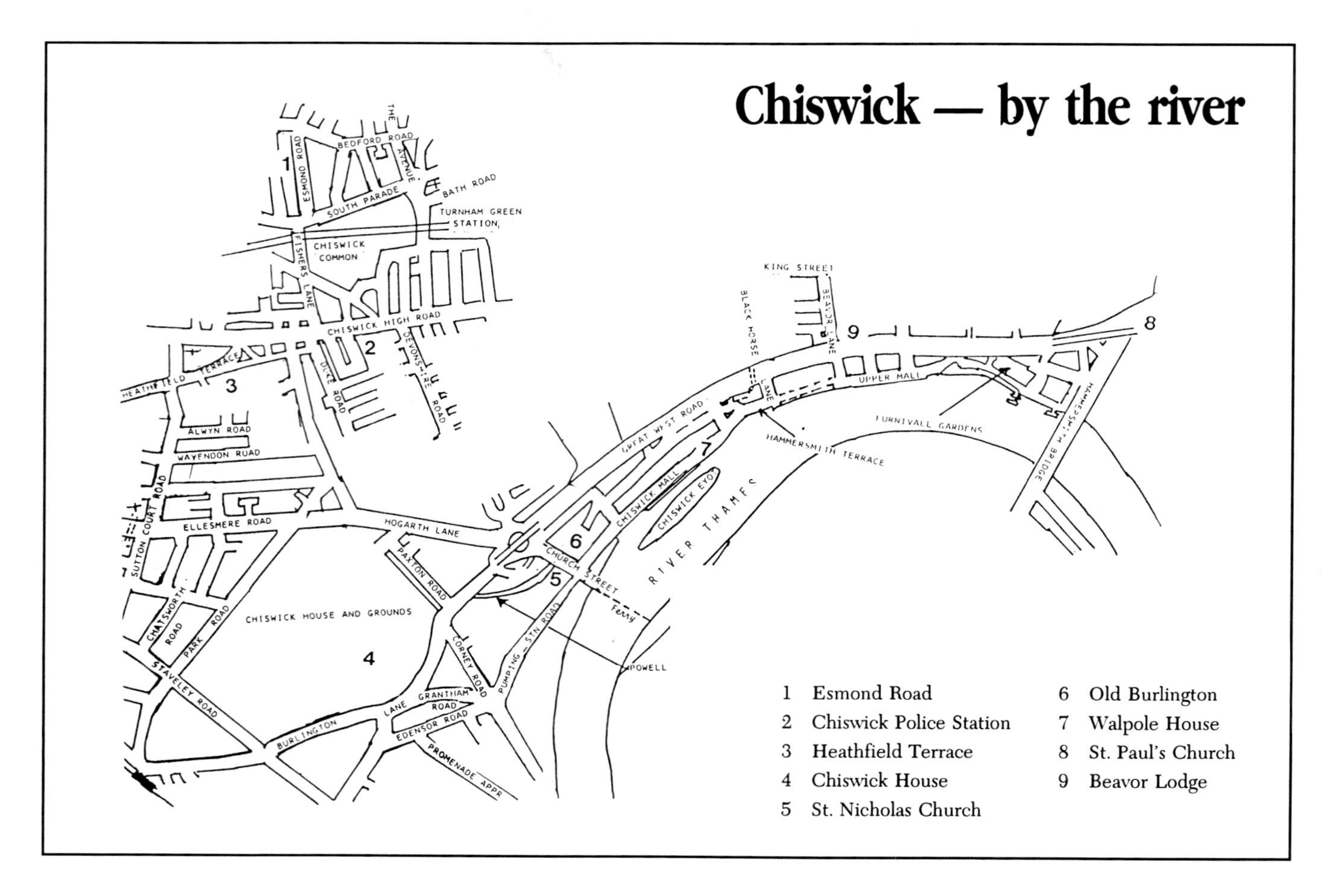

1 Esmond Road
2 Chiswick Police Station
3 Heathfield Terrace
4 Chiswick House
5 St. Nicholas Church
6 Old Burlington
7 Walpole House
8 St. Paul's Church
9 Beavor Lodge

Walk 1:
Chiswick — by the river

Distance: 3·5 miles.

Route: Turnham Green Underground Station – The Avenue – Bedford Road – Esmond Road – Heathfield Terrace – Sutton Court Road – Staveley Road – Burlington Lane – Church Street – Chiswick Mall – Upper Mall – Furnivall Gardens – Hammersmith Broadway – Hammersmith Underground Station.

Public transport: Starting at Turnham Green Underground Station on the District and Piccadilly Lines — Buses 94 and E3.
Finishing at Hammersmith Underground Station on the District and Piccadilly Lines — Buses 9, 9A, 10, 27, 33, 72, 190 and 211.

Refreshments: There are a number of fast-food establishments along Chiswick High Road. In Chiswick House grounds there is a refreshment place. Along the riverside there are a number of public houses, most of whom serve food as well as drink, in particular the Black Horse, in the lane by that name. On the Upper Mall can be found the Old Ship (Hammersmith's oldest public house) and further on The Dove, and Rutland. All have full views of the river. Be warned on Boat Race day they get very very crowded! Once back into Hammersmith there are numerous eating places.

ROUTE DIRECTIONS

On leaving the entrance to the station turn right and walk along to The Avenue and then left along Bedford Road. At the end of the latter roadway is Esmond Street. Turn left and walk down to (1). At the road junction cross over South Parade and walk down Fishers Lane, passing under the railway bridge, this leads to Chiswick High Road. Turn left, cross the road and on the corner of Linden Gardens is the Chiswick Police Station (2). Continue to walk along the High Road towards Heathfield Terrace (3). After leaving this point of the walk proceed to Sutton Court Road and, where the road crosses Ellesmere Road, use the subway to continue walking down Sutton Court Road. At Staveley Road turn left and walk to Burlington Lane at the end is the entrance to the grounds of Chiswick House (4). On leaving the grounds turn left, walk along to Paxton Road, cross Burlington Lane by way of the pedestrian crossing, and along Burlington Lane to Church

Street (5) (6). At the far end of Church Street is Chiswick Mall, is a pleasant riverside walk. But beware if it is high tide as the river constantly overflows its banks here and floods the Mall. You could be walking along the road accompanied by a swan or two! Do not approach, or try to feed, them as they can be extremely vicious. Ahead is Walpole House (7). Just past the house is Hammersmith Terrace, a direct continuation of Chiswick Mall, which leads behind the houses that back directly on to the riverside. A short walk along the terrace is Black Horse Lane leading to the Great West Road. This makes an appropriate point of the walk to digress to visit the site at the end of Beavor Lane (9). Care however should be taken to use the subway under the Great West Road to visit the site. Returning to the terrace the riverside walk resumes as Upper Mall that leads to Furnivall Gardens and Hammersmith Bridge. Turn left and walk along Hammersmith Bridge Road, carefully crossing under the Hammersmith Flyover to reach the Parish Church of St. Paul Hammersmith (8). For those not wishing to make a diversion along Black Horse Lane to Beavor Lane (9) a visit to the site can now be made by walking along to it from the side of the flyover.

POINTS OF INTEREST

1. ESMOND ROAD

There have been a number of hauntings reported from time to time throughout London in council houses or flats including one where razor blades travelled through the air. Here in Esmond Road during July 1956 was the scene of some extraordinary happenings when pennies struck the inhabitants across the face, were dislodged in an empty room, and, when collected up others appeared. One boy in particular seemed to attract these coins, and other items of metal, towards his person, so it was decided to send him away to relatives in Essex. During the time he was away from the family home the poltergeist seems to have found another home, and has not been heard or seen of since.

2. CHISWICK POLICE STATION

In Chiswick's Police Station, in the High Road, there is another ghost from a previous house on the site. The station stands on the site of the former Linden House, built in the eighteenth century, where in the cellars a Mrs Abercrombie, murdered her son-in-law with a meat chopper, whose ghost is said to be still attempting to escape her blows.

3. HEATHFIELD TERRACE

Over the past two hundred years this site has been home to a variety of buildings including an army barracks, a furniture warehouse, and more recently the latter has been converted into flats. Before the spread of housing, and other buildings, the building served as a landmark both from the road and from the river. Today, aircraft passing on their way to and from London Airport (Heathrow) use it as a turning point for their flight. During its time as a furniture storage place there were several observations made by members of the staff of the second floor being haunted. Several porters refused to go into these rooms while others claimed that an exorcist should be brought in to clear the matter up. One man claimed having seen an old man walking through a locked door, another saw a man lurking around some of the stored pieces of furniture. When he called to him he disappeared.

4. CHISWICK HOUSE'S VILLA

Although the kitchens have long since been removed from the old Chiswick House, and all that remains today is the Chiswick Villa, built by Lord Burlington to house his collection of objet-d'arts, there have been many reports of the aroma of frying eggs and bacon. The only part of the house left today is the former link building between the house and the villa. The house was used at the turn of the century as a summer country house by Edward, Prince of Wales, later Edward VII and his children are said to have told this story to the guests at the house.

5. PARISH CHURCH OF ST. NICHOLAS

The medieval church of St. Nicholas, Chiswick was rebuilt in the nineteenth century, and while most of the memorials from the previous church were transferred, the grave of two of Oliver Cromwell's daughters were left unmarked. Buried anonymously for fear of reprisals by Royalists their ghosts were seen walking about the church at the time of the rebuilding.

6. OLD BURLINGTON PUBLIC HOUSE

Although it has long ceased to be a public house, the Old Burlington, opposite the parish church of St. Nicholas Chiswick, still has a regular customer, Percy. With his wide brimmed black hat and cloak he has been described as "of good humour and harmless". While traditionally it is said that Dick Turpin once leapt from an upper room on to the waiting back of Black Bess, there has never been any suggestion that Percy is a pseudonym for the notorious highway man.

Old Burlington Public House

Walpole House, The Mall

7. WALPOLE HOUSE, THE MALL

Although not strictly a royal residence, Walpole House, on the Chiswick Mall, has distinct royal connections in that a mistress of Charles II, Barbara, Duchess of Cleveland, a great beauty in her time, lived and died here in 1709. At certain times of the year the tap-tap of the heels of her shoes can be heard moving up and down the staircase of the house. On moonlit nights she peers from the window of one of the upper rooms, bewailing her lost looks and the loss of the King to another. The Duchess died in 1709, and lies buried in the nearby parish church of St. Nicholas.

8. PARISH CHURCH OF ST. PAUL, HAMMERSMITH

Seen rising from an old tombstone in St. Paul's churchyard was a tall white apparition, the ghost of a suicide who ended his life long before the present church building was erected. The foundation stone for the church was laid in 1882, and the church consecrated in the late nineteenth century. The church replaced the former chapel of ease which dated from 1611. In the nineteenth century the ghost was recorded as having chased a young girl through the churchyard, but as it caught up with her — she fainted. In order to way-lay and expose this particular spirit, a number of local inhabitants organised a vigilante group, but tragedy struck when one of them, seeing a white figure, fired a shot. It was a white-coated workman returning late from his toil using the churchyard as a short cut home. The vigils were abandoned, the culprit tried for murder, found guilty, and sentenced to death. However, the sentence was commuted and he only served one year of his sentence in prison. In the following year, 1804, a passing stagecoach was held up by the ghost, the driver promptly abandoned his post, the horses bolted, and only good fortune saved the coach from plunging into the River Thames.

9. Beavor Lodge, Beavor Lane

Connecting King Street with the Great West Road is Hammersmith's Beavor Lane. Here stood Beavor Lodge where the sounds of a woman crying often disturbed the local residents by day and night. A tall grey-clothed lady is seen walking through the house and has been identified as an informer who, when caught by her accomplices, was taken in a large sack and drowned in the nearby river. Several members of the servants' household are reported to have seen her in the last century and to have fainted from fright. A second explanation as to the origin of the lady was given after a seance was held to ascertain the reason for her presence. The medium told the people present that she was a nun who had given birth to a child and buried it in the garden of the lodge. When the artist William Richmond and his family lived here in the 1870s they told their friends of strange noises in the night, and of doors being opened without their handles being touched, with long sighs being heard at all hours of the day and night.

Chiswick House

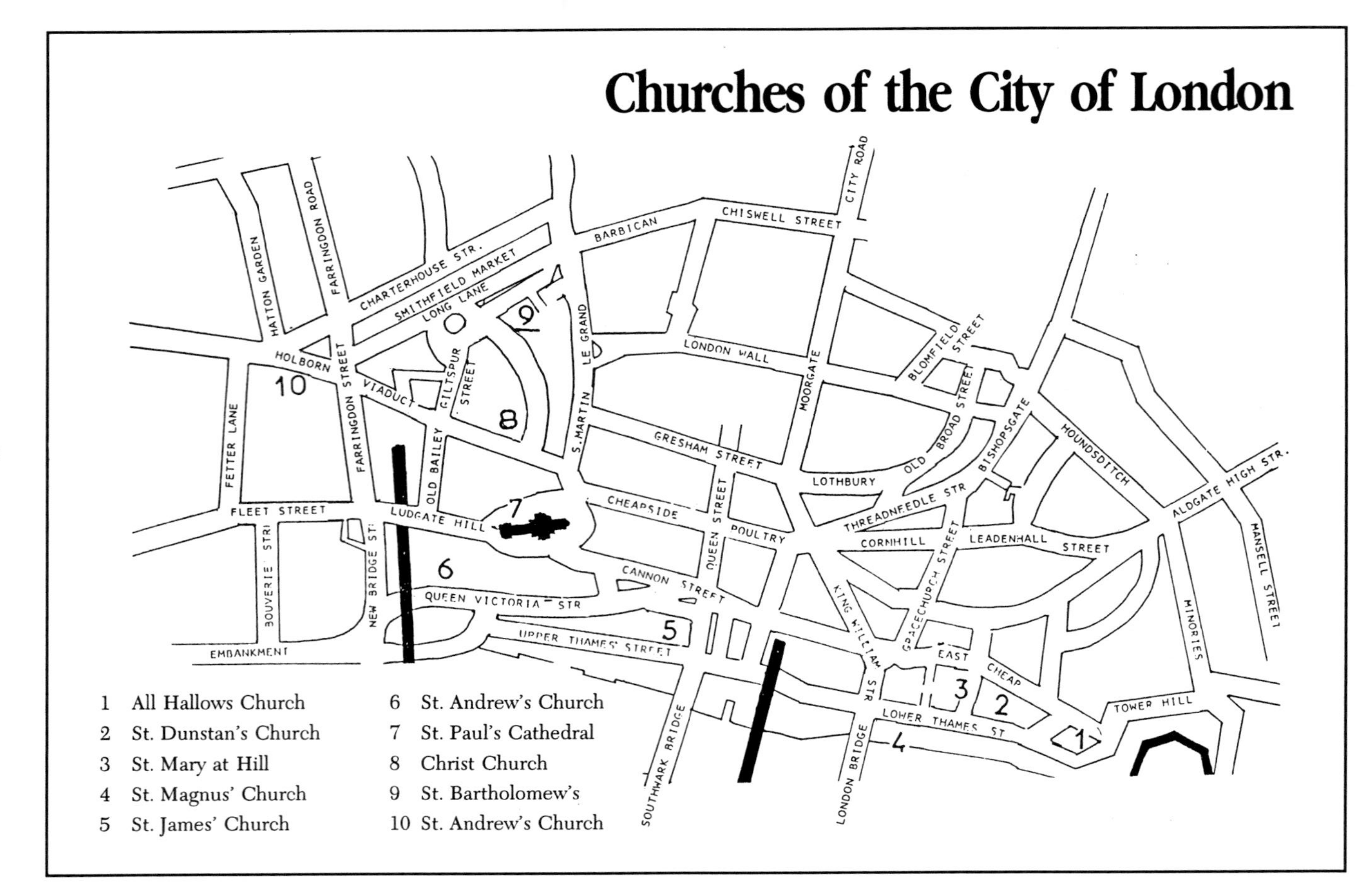
Churches of the City of London
HATTON GARDEN
FARRINGDON ROAD
CHARTERHOUSE STR.
SMITHFIELD MARKET
LONG LANE
BARBICAN
CHISWELL STREET
CITY ROAD
HOLBORN
FARRINGDON STREET
VIADUCT
GILTSPUR STREET
LE GRAND
S.MARTIN
LONDON WALL
MOORGATE
BLOMFIELD STREET
OLD BROAD STREET
BISHOPSGATE
HOUNDSDITCH
ALDGATE HIGH STR.
MANSELL STREET
MINORIES
FETTER LANE
FLEET STREET
OLD BAILEY
LUDGATE HILL
GRESHAM STREET
LOTHBURY
THREADNEEDLE STR
CHEAPSIDE
QUEEN STREET
POULTRY
CORNHILL
LEADENHALL STREET
GRACECHURCH STREET
CANNON STREET
KING WILLIAM STR
EAST CHEAP
TOWER HILL
BOUVERIE STR
NEW BRIDGE STR
QUEEN VICTORIA STR
UPPER THAMES STREET
EMBANKMENT
SOUTHWARK BRIDGE
LONDON BRIDGE
LOWER THAMES ST
1 All Hallows Church
2 St. Dunstan's Church
3 St. Mary at Hill
4 St. Magnus' Church
5 St. James' Church
6 St. Andrew's Church
7 St. Paul's Cathedral
8 Christ Church
9 St. Bartholomew's
10 St. Andrew's Church

Walk 2: Churches of the City of London

Distance: 1·75 miles

Route: Tower Hill Underground Station – All Hallows-by-the-Tower – St. Dunstan-in-the-East – St. Mary-at-Hill – St. Magnus-the-Martyr – St. James Garlickhithe – St. Andrew-by-the-Wardrobe – St. Paul's Cathedral – Christ Church Newgate Street – St. Bartholomew-the-Great – St. Andrew Holborn.

Public transport: Starting at Tower Hill Underground Station on the Circle and District Lines — Buses 15, 15A, 25, 42, 7, 100, D1, D9 and 511
Finishing at Chancery Lane Underground Station on the Central Line — Buses 17, 22B, 25, 45, 46, 171A, 501 and 511

Refreshments: Weekdays numerous, fewer at weekends.

ROUTE DIRECTIONS

From the Underground station cross Trinity Square to the Parish Church of All Hallows-by-the-Tower (1), On leaving the church turn left and cross under the road by way of the subway emerging on the corner of Byward and Great Tower Street. Walk along to St. Dunstan's Hill to the former Parish Church of St. Dunstan-in-the-East. Walk along St. Dunstan's Lane. Cross over St. Mary-at-Hill. Pass under the archway — with its skull and crossbones — to the entrance of St. Mary-at-Hill Parish Church (3). Walk down Lovat Lane to Monument Street and Lower Thames Street. Turn right and walk along to the traffic lights opposite the Parish Church of St. Magnus the Martyr. Cross over the roadway to the church (4). From the church, walk under London Bridge to Queen Street Place. Cross the road to Queen Street on the left-hand side is Skinners Lane at the end of which is the Parish Church of St. James Garlickhithe (5). Walk up Garlick Hill to Queen Victoria Street. Turn left and walk along to the second pedestrian crossing. Cross the road and turn left to walk along to the Parish Church of St. Andrew-by-the-Wardrobe (6). St. Andrews Hill leads to Carter Lane, turn right to Dean's Court. At the end of the lane is St. Paul's Cathedral (7). On the north side of the cathedral is St. Paul's Underground Station and Newgate Street. Turn left and walk along to the pedestrian crossing. Cross to the ruined Christ Church (8). Leave the gardens and walk along to Smithfield by way of King Edward Street and Little Britain. Here is the Priory Church of St. Bartholomew the Great (9), Leave Smithfield by Giltspur Street and on reaching the Parish Church of St. Sepulchre-without-Newgate turn right to the Guild Church of St. Andrew Holborn (10). From the church it is a short walk to Chancery Lane Underground Station. [Central Line].

POINTS OF INTEREST

1. Parish Church of All-Hallows-by-the-Tower

In the seventeenth century there was a fire in a chandler's shop in the parish that reduced it to ashes, and killed the occupants. Later that day, however, a parishioner passing by the church heard the whimpering of a small child. Investigating the noise led members of the church to search the roof of the building — and found a baby. She was identified as being the youngest member of the chandler's family. She was cared for by relatives and was later married in the church. She has never been seen but her babyish cries have been heard coming from the north roof of the church.

During the period between the two World Wars of this century another ghost has been recorded as making an appearance from time to time — a fine Persian cat. The owner of the cat was the organist of the church Miss Liscette Rist, who had been refused permission to have her cat buried in the churchyard after its death. No sightings have been recorded since the church has been rebuilt after war damage.

2. Parish Church of St. Dunstan-in-the-East

Now a pleasant oasis surrounded by offices having been laid out as a garden after plans to restore it were abandoned. During the Second World War, 1939–45, the church was bombed at a time when the crypt was being used as an air-raid shelter. It is from those latter days that the ghost of the church emulates. An old lady is sometimes seen, complete with her wartime gas mask and case, wandering down the hill towards Lower Thames Street and, hopefully, safety.

3. Parish Church of St. Mary-at-Hill

During restoration work in the nineteenth century the foundations of the church were exposed for a short time. The graves of Richard and Alice Hackney were found. Their coffins had almost rotted away but the body of Alice was said to have been in such perfect condition that it was put on display for four days before being placed in a new coffin and reburied. Unfortunately, it was not replaced in the same position as it had been found, since which time her restless ghost has been searching for her lost husband's grave.

4. Parish Church of St. Magnus the Martyr

Here, on a number of occasions, a man dressed in a black cassock, the robe of a priest or server, has been seen in the north aisle of the church. A former verger, alone in the church late one winter's afternoon, approached a figure that he took to be a priest and asked if he could be of any service to him — the figure simply faded away before his eyes. On another occasion a church worker sewing in the vestry became aware that someone had entered the church through, she thought, the west door. She left her work to investigate, but found the church empty. A young child entered the church asked to leave immediately. "It's cold in here mummy" said she. The heating was full on at the time! Who can this ghost be? It is likely to be Miles Coverdale, Bishop of Exeter, 1551–53, the famous reformer, who revised Tyndale's translation of the Bible. He was Rector of the parish, 1563–66, and also became associated with the former Parish of St. Bartholomew-by-the-Exchange, where he was originally buried. When the church was demolished in 1841 to make room for extensions to the Bank of England his body was transferred to St. Magnus's church. It is his restless spirit that wanders around the church.

5. Parish Church of St. James Garlickhithe

Workmen in the nineteenth century engaged in restoration work of the choir stalls discovered a complete skeleton of a man. His identity remained a mystery until another restoration programme in the 1990s revealed that he was a seventeenth-century sailor. For many years he stood upright in a cupboard in the vestibule of the church locked away from the prying eyes of the twentieth century. He now has a new "home" in a room in the tower. Shortly after being found he is said to have been observed by visitors to the church. Sometimes he is covered with a shroud (burial cloth), with his hands crossed over his chest. He never speaks, but stops and stares at whoever is in the church, then gradually fades away. During the Second World War a fireman patrolling the church saw a dark figure during an air-raid, and suggested that he took shelter nearby — but it simply faded away before the man's eyes. After the War an American tourist and her two sons were exploring the church one afternoon when the elder of the two saw a man. By the time that he had managed to get the attention of his mother and younger brother, the vision had faded away. It is not recorded whether the family had seen the mummified figure earlier during their visit and that the boy may have imagined what he thought he had seen.

6. Parish Church of St. Andrew-by-the-Wardrobe

The suffix derives from the proximity of the King's Great Wardrobe, or storehouse, close by until its destruction in the Great Fire of 1666. In 1933 from the ruined church of Avenbury, in Herefordshire, the church bought three medieval church bells. Legend attributes to these bells the habit of ringing, unaided, on the deathbed of the Rector of their former Parish. The largest of the three bells now rests in the vestibule of the church, weighs 11cwt, and bears the inscription in Latin reading "I have the name of Gabriel sent from Heaven".

Parish Church of St. Andrew-by-the-Wardrobe

7. St. Paul's Cathedral

The present, third, building on the site was designed by Sir Christopher Wren after the Great Fire of 1666. Here a whistling ghost follows members of the staff around the building. In particular it seems to be attracted to the north-west corner chapel where it whistles the loudest and then it disappears into the wall. In the same chapel — All Souls or Kitchener Memorial Chapel — a strange luminous patch has appeared on the wall. Gradually the form takes the shape of a priest dressed in clerical robes. It is only visible for a few seconds then it disappears from sight.

8. Christ Church, Newgate Street

The site was the former church of the Greyfriars monastic establishment, a branch of the Order of St. Francis of Assisi. After the Dissolution of the Monasteries in the sixteenth century part of the building was used as a Parish Church. Rebuilt after the Great Fire, by Wren, it was later severely damaged during the last war. Today it is a "maintain ruin", with a beautiful rose garden on the site of the church. Here was buried in 1384 Edward II's Queen Isabella who, after his murder, ruled in his place for a short time. On her death she left instructions that the heart of her husband should be buried in the same coffin as herself. Her ghost is said to have been joined by that of the Fair Maid of Kent who was executed at Tyburn in 1534 for opposing Henry VIII's marriage to Anne Boleyn and his divorce from Catherine of Arragon. The Maid forecast that the king would lose his throne if he should remarry — he did but didn't! A third body, that of Lady Hungerford, executed at Tyburn for poisoning her husband, also lies buried here. Her ghost has been seen but she never talks to the other ghosts! Recent rebuilding works in the immediate area seems to have quietened all three ghosts as there have not been any reported sightings since the early 1950s. Other reported sightings here have included a figure clothed in a russet brown habit. He has been seen in the early hours of late summer mornings, but disappears at daybreak. When the Franciscan Friars first arrived in England in the thirteenth century brown was the colour of their clothing. But to whom did the little dog belong that has been seen jumping around the churchyard?

9. PARISH CHURCH OF ST. BARTHOLOMEW THE GREAT

Built originally in the twelfth century by Rahere as the Priory Church for Augustinian Canons. After the Dissolution it became the parish church serving the people of Smithfield. Many a level-headed person has felt or seen the presence of the supernatural in the church. All agree that a black-robed figure has appeared to them and that footsteps have been heard in an otherwise silent church. Who is this ghost? Rahere. His ghostly appearances have been recorded over the years and include the lady who was arranging the flowers near the high altar, which despite her desperate efforts would not stay in the vase. This has been attributed to Rahere's dislike of women (!) and to the voiceless Rahere standing in the pulpit attempting to preach from it. There is also a second ghost, a "nasty, fearful, black shape" which envelops certain people entering the church, some of whom have fled in horror, never to return. This ghostly apparition has not been seen for some time and it is assumed to have moved on to another place. Rahere has also been seen in St. Bartholomew's Hospital across the way from the entrance to the church.

10. ST. ANDREW'S GUILD CHURCH, HOLBORN CIRCUS

Although the church escaped destruction in the Great Fire it was rebuilt by Wren in 1686. Some ghosts have drawn crowds of people to watch their nightly performances and one such apparition appeared on the streets of London in September 1815 near St. Andrew's Church. Alarm is reported to have spread over the days at the beginning of the month because of the antics of the ghost. Large crowds gathered to see the sight, at nine o'clock they were rewarded for their waiting. But when the cry of the ghost filled the air, most of the people ran away in fright. A small and more determined band of parishioners stayed and watched the display of acrobatics. Some of the more daring members of the crowd moved forward closer toward the ghost but "it" leapt over the back railings of the churchyard — disappeared — and was never seen again!

A Haunted City of London

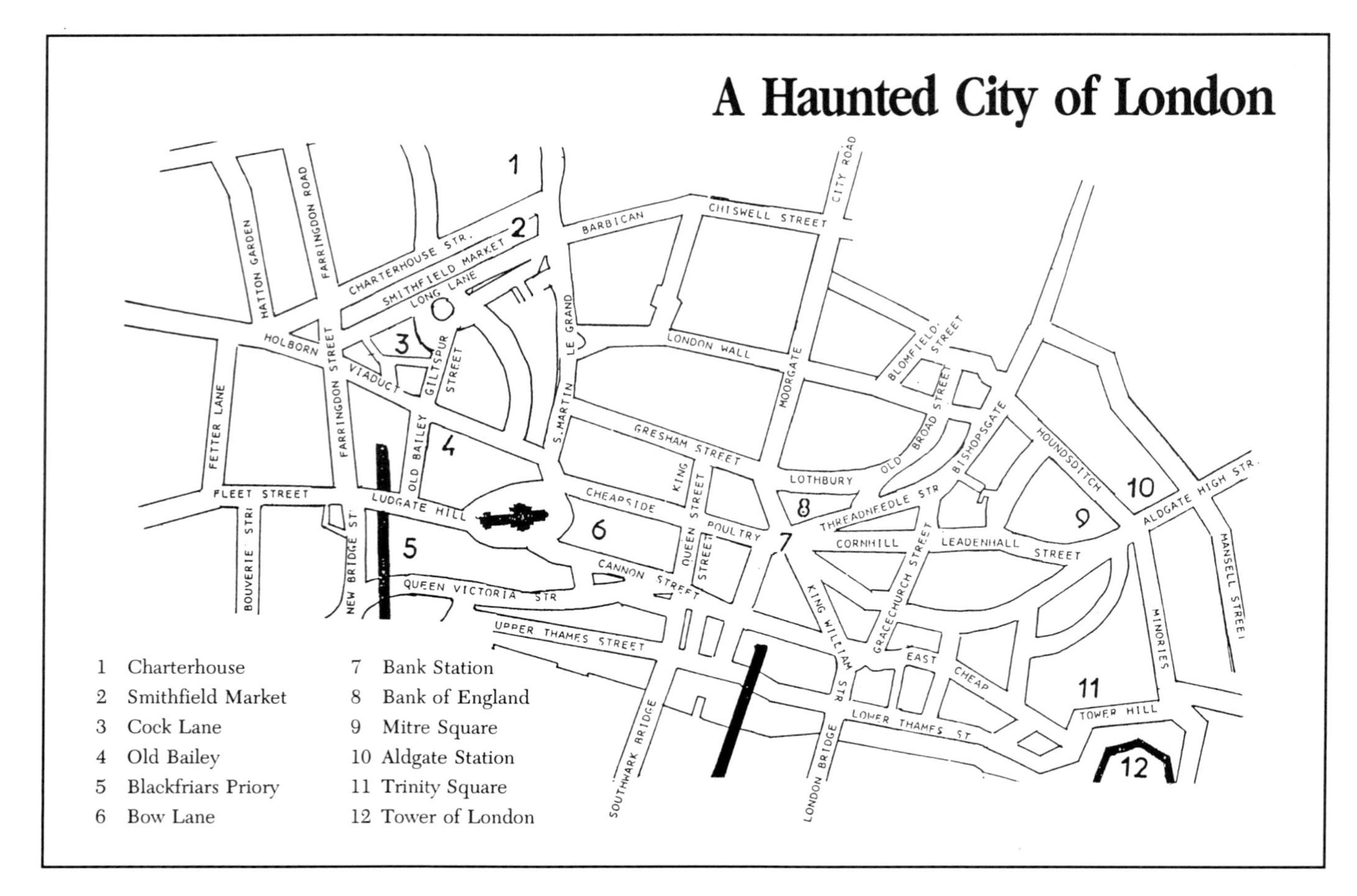

1 Charterhouse
2 Smithfield Market
3 Cock Lane
4 Old Bailey
5 Blackfriars Priory
6 Bow Lane
7 Bank Station
8 Bank of England
9 Mitre Square
10 Aldgate Station
11 Trinity Square
12 Tower of London

Walk 3:
A Haunted City of London

Distance: 1·75 miles

Route: Barbican Underground Station – Carthusian Street – Charterhouse Street – Smithfield Market – Long Lane – Giltspur Street – Cock Lane – Newgate – Blackfriars Priory – Groveland Court, off Bow Lane – Bank Station – Threadneedle Street – Cornhill – Leadenhall Street – Mitre Square – Aldgate High Street – Aldgate Station – Minories – Tower Hill – Tower of London.

Public Transport: Starting at Barbican Underground Station on the Circle, Hammersmith and City Lines — Buses 4, 56 and 172
Finishing at Tower Hill Underground Station on the Circle and District Lines — Buses 15 and 25

Refreshments: Weekdays — a number of public houses, snack bars and fast-food establishments on the route, but limited at weekends.

ROUTE DIRECTIONS

At the entrance to the Underground station turn right and walk along Aldersgate Street to Carthusian Street that leads to Charterhouse Square (1). Leave the square and return to Charterhouse Street and walk along Smithfield Central Meat Market (2) and its Grand Avenue. At the further end of the avenue to Smithfield, cross Long Lane and walk round the area, past the entrance to St. Bartholomew's Hospital and leave Smithfield by way of Giltspur Street. Standing high on the corner of Cock Lane (3) is the little naked boy who marks one of the extremes of the Great Fire of London. At the end of the lane turn left and walk up Snow Hill to the Holborn Viaduct. On the corner of the Old Bailey stands the Central Criminal Courts (4) whose dome is dominated by the figure of Justice holding a pair of scales in one hand and the sword of Justice in the other. Walk down the Old Bailey, cross Ludgate Hill, and continue walking through Pageant Master's Court, and Broadway until Carter Lane is reached. Turn left along the lane to Church Entry (5). Return to Carter Lane, turn right, and walk to Dean's Court Ahead is St. Paul's Cathedral. Walk along the south side of the cathedral and then Cannon Street to Bow Lane (on the left hand side). In Bow Lane, on the left is Groveland Court, and Williamson's Tavern (6). Continue up Bow Lane, past the east end of St. Mary Le Bow Parish Church to Cheapside, turn right. Walk ahead, by way of Poultry to The Bank. The station (7) has numerous entrances and exits one of which allows the walker to cross over this complex road junction in safety. Using the appropriate exit you will arrive at the Bank of England (8) from here the route is by way of Cornhill and Leadenhall Street to Mitre Square (9). On leaving the square cross the Houndsditch, again by using the pedestrian subway and emerge at Aldgate High Street, close by the Parish Church of St. Botolph Aldgate. Nearby is Aldgate Underground Station (10). Cross Aldgate High Street and walk down the Minories to Tower Hill (11) from here across the road can be seen the Tower of London (12).

POINTS OF INTEREST

1. CHARTERHOUSE, CHARTERHOUSE SQUARE

Charterhouse was the London home of the monastic Order of Carthusians and was founded in 1372 by Walter Manny on ground that was known as Pardon Churchyard. It was dissolved at the time of the Dissolution of the Monasteries in the sixteenth century, and eventually bought by Thomas Sutton who endowed a school, and almshouses for eighty men Pensioners. Several ghosts have recorded appearances here. Among them is a head of a duke thought to be that of the 4th Duke of Norfolk who once lived here. He was beheaded on instructions from Elizabeth I who took exception to his proposal of marriage to Mary Queen of Scots. Earlier in this century workmen at work in the Great Chamber became aware of a third presence. When they approached him he disappeared! The workmen never worked alone in the chamber after that. Charterhouse is not open to the general public but group visits can be arranged. There will be an admission fee.

2. SMITHFIELD MEAT MARKET, WEST SMITHFIELD

One of the most notorious sites in the whole of London — Smithfield is known throughout the world for the great meat market carried on there since the twelfth century. It is the smooth-field outside the City Wall. Here, in 1303, was executed William Wallace the Scottish Patriot, while in the sixteenth century a cook of the Bishop of Rochester was boiled alive for poisoning a number of the Bishop's guests. It is hardly surprising that passers-by late at night are said to have heard the cries of these unfortunates echoing across the empty space in front of the market buildings. One or two have claimed to have smelt the burning flesh of others who were burnt alive here for the Faith during the times of persecution of the sixteenth and seventeenth centuries. In 1538 the Prior of the Observant Convent of Greenwich was roasted alive here for denying the Supremacy of Henry VIII. John Rogers and other Protestant martyrs were also burnt alive here and their cries are said to have reached out into the twentieth century. The market building itself has had its fair share of ghosts including one who is said to disturb the huge carcasses of meat they used to hang from hooks inside the building.

3. 20 COCK LANE, REBUILT 1979

Perhaps one of the most popular ghosts of the City of London is that of Cock Lane. The story begins with the death in 1757 of the wife of William Kent. After her death Kent went to live with his sister-in-law, Fanny, in Cock Lane in a house that was owned by Thomas Parsons a clerk of St. Sepulchre's church nearby. Strange noises were heard by Fanny who at first, attributed them to noisy neighbours, but later identified them as coming from her sister. They were taken as protests from Fanny's sister from the grave and ceased after William and Fanny moved to Clerkenwell. The noises returned after Fanny's death from smallpox in 1760. In the eighteenth century Horace Walpole was one of the many sightseers who visited the house, and sat around the bed from where these strange noises came. Over the years all major religions have claimed Fanny's sister as being "one of them" and have emphasised the perils of living in sin.

4. Central Criminal Courts, (Newgate Prison)

On the site of the former Newgate Prison stands the Central Criminal Courts — the Old Bailey. The present courts were built in 1902 when the notorious Newgate Prison was pulled down. Here, in the old prison in very cramped conditions all types of criminals were housed. Over the years the site witnessed a number of ghostly apparitions. The archives reveal how once a prison officer, working late at his desk, near Dead Man's Walk, heard a noise and went off to investigate. He was confronted by a face looking through the grille that led into the Walk. On opening the door the face disappeared and all that he heard was the slow shuffle of a lame person walking away. One Chaplain was preparing the chapel for morning service when he was disturbed by a noise from behind the screen of the condemned cell. On opening the door of the screen he saw a gentleman dressed in a black coat wearing a powdered wig. Some time later, in another place, the chaplain saw a portrait of Henry Fauntleroy who had been executed at Newgate for forgery. It was the same man. Dead Man's Walk was the most haunted of all the places in the prison. Part of the walk now forms a wall at the rear of Amen Court, in Ave Maria Lane (the lane runs parallel with the Old Bailey). The court is the private property of the Dean and Chapter of St. Paul's Cathedral and may not be visited. However, the wall can be seen from the public roadway of the lane. It was in the Walk that Mrs Dyer died, who ran a baby-minding service, and who murdered her charges by throwing them into the River Thames. Tried, and found guilty for her heinous crimes she was sentenced to be hanged. On her way to the gallows she swore that she would return. She did, and haunted the warden who had escorted her to the gallows. Suddenly while he was walking through the exercise yard of the prison a large black form confronted him, and gradually took the shape of Mrs Dyer. She had kept her promise. A Minor Canon of St. Paul's, living in Amen Court during the 1950s, always claimed that he saw Jack Shepherd, the highwayman, creeping along the top of the wall making one of his numerous escapes from the prison. According to the records of Newgate Prison he has also been seen, well-fettered, deep in the Underground cells of the Central Criminal Courts.

5. Blackfriars Priory

When Eleanor of Castille, the first wife of Edward I, died in 1291 her body was embalmed by nuns in Lincoln. Everywhere her body rested for the night on its journey from Lincoln to London the king ordered that a memorial cross should be erected, the penultimate cross being in Cheapside. Here the Queen's heart, that had been separately embalmed and placed in a silver container was removed and buried in the Blackfriars Priory. Recent building upheavals in the area seem to have disturbed the queen's heart and she has been seen among the ruins of the last church on the site.

6. GROVELAND COURT, OFF BOW LANE

It is not only humans who are afraid of ghostly scenes and atmospheres; animals too are sensitive as may be recorded in Groveland Court, off Bow Lane. A City policeman was patrolling the area with his dog who could not be persuaded to enter the court for fear. It seems that some dogs are more prone to be upset by an "atmosphere" than others. When the new tenant of a nearby public house brought his dog into the City one day it showed no fear at all.

Groveland Court

7. BANK UNDERGROUND STATION

At the busy Bank Station, where many lines converge and an escalator links with the Monument Station a pungent smell rising from certain areas has been reported. It has been linked to a smell coming from an open grave. A possible explanation is that the station and its many tunnels passes near to, or through, a disused graveyard or plague pit of one of the lost churches of the City.

8. THE BANK OF ENGLAND

When "resurrectionists" — men who robbed the grave of newly buried persons — were fully active in the City a cashier was worried that his body would be removed from its grave after death. Realising the security of The Bank, he sought and obtained permission to be buried within its walls — a fact recorded in The Bank's archives. His coffin is still in situ. In spite of all due precautions, being buried in a lead covered coffin and bound with heavy chains, his restless ghost can be seen walking the corridors of The Bank. The centre courtyard of The Bank is a very pleasant garden that has been haunted by Sarah Whitehead since the nineteenth century. Her brother, Philip, who was employed at The Bank was arrested, found guilty of forgery and hanged. Sarah refused to accept either his guilt or his death, and regularly visited the building and asked to see him. She continued to do so for over thirty years and on her death was buried in the churchyard of St. Christopher Le Stocks. The present building covers the site of the church and its churchyard. So, she can still visit and ask for her brother — which she does from time to time!

9. Mitre Square

Although Mitre Square has been rebuilt and all traces of the former warehouses have been removed the site remains haunted. Here, while returning home early in the morning of 30th September 1888, Catherine Eddows, a local prostitute, was accosted by a man. Thinking that he might be a client she stopped. He turned out to be "Jack the Ripper". Her heavily mutilated body was found later that morning by a policeman returning to his station in Bishopsgate. A ghostly form has been seen lying in the corner of the square by persons using the square as a short cut to the nearby Underground station. She was last seen in 1980 when the last warehouse was being demolished to make way for extra playing space for the school here.

10. Aldgate Underground Station

Nestling just outside the City Wall is Aldgate Underground station where a number of ghosts have been reported and officially entered into the station's log. Footsteps have been heard coming from the sleepers — the wooden supports for the lines along which the trains run — as if a track man is checking the lines for safety reasons. In the early 1950s an engineer at the station saw an old woman stroking the hair of a colleague. Unaware of the incident at the time, the colleague shortly afterwards made a fatal mistake, resulting in 22,000 volts of electricity passing through his body. Although knocked unconscious he lived to tell the story and always thanked the old lady for acting as his 'earth' to the impulse. Whistling has also been heard coming from the station's platform area, although deserted at the time.

11. Trinity Square Gardens, Tower Hill

Sandwiched between the Tower of London and the boundary of the City of London are the Trinity Square Gardens where can be seen the site of the scaffold that was erected for public executions. The solemn procession would start from the Tower of London and lead the victims to their death at the hands of the public executioner. A sentry on duty at the main gate of the Tower of London in 1940 witnessed a stately procession of priests, soldiers and other persons dressed in the clothes of another age. He called the Officer of the Watch but by the time he arrived they had vanished. Around the site today are listed some of the more famous, and infamous, persons to be beheaded here.

12. TOWER OF LONDON

A site within the Tower was normally used only for "private" executions and for persons whose death might be prevented by loyal supporters. Many of these victims have returned in a supernatural form. Among these is a figure dressed in a long black velvet dress with a white cap on her head. It is thought to be Lady Jane Grey who is known as "Jane, nine days to reign" who succeeded Edward VI to the throne but who did not get enough support to sustain her position. She is seen in and around the Bloody and Salt Towers. Anne Boleyn, Henry VIII's second wife wanders around Tower Green — the site of the execution block — as well as the nearby White Tower. More than one soldier has seen a short procession of pall-bearers carrying a large arrow box on their shoulders towards the Church of St. Peter ad Vincula where the queen lies buried before the high altar. There being no proper coffin available, after her execution her body was placed in the arrow box. One of the most cruel executions was that of Margaret, Countess of Salisbury, mother of Cardinal Archbishop Reginald Pole, the last Roman Catholic Archbishop. She protested her innocence, and although nearly seventy years of age at the time had to be chased around the block before being caught and led up the scaffold. The axeman struck five times before severing her head from her shoulders. Her screams still pierce the still night within the Tower. Lady Jane Grey's father, the Duke of Northumberland, takes his ghostly walk between the Martin and Constable Towers. Sir Walter Raleigh has been seen looking over the river walk by the Bloody Tower where he was imprisoned for thirteen years. Perhaps he meets the ghosts of the two young princes who were murdered there in the fifteenth century. Footsteps have been heard in various places within the walls of the Tower including the Governor's House. Daytime visitors have also been recorded. One such incident occurred when a warder was working in the White Tower and saw a woman looking in a showcase at the time when the Tower was closed to members of the public. Henry VI is said to visit the Wakefield Tower on the eve of the anniversary of his murder, 21st May. On the day itself flowers appear "mysteriously" on the site of his death. After dark the Tower can be a very "spooky" place to wander around. Built in the thirteenth century the Martin Tower housed the Royal Regalia in the latter half of the seventeenth century. It has been used previously to house prisoners of the State, including Queen Anne Boleyn, and Thomas Percy one of the conspirators of the Gunpowder Plot. Both these persons have been seen in and around the Tower. In the nineteenth century their appearance was so frequent that guards would only patrol in pairs in the vicinity.

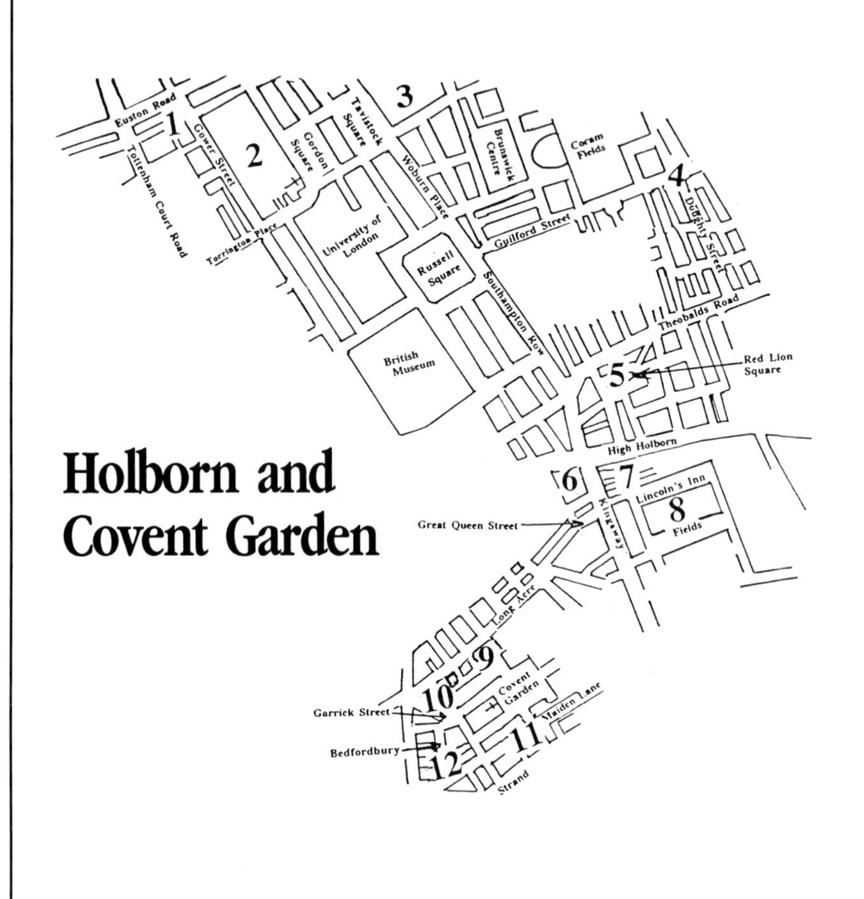

Holborn and Covent Garden

1 Gower Street
2 University College
3 Tavistock Place
4 Doughty Street
5 Red Lion Square
6 Holy Trinity Church
7 Ship Tavern, Gate Street
8 Lincoln's Inn Fields
9 Covent Garden Station
10 Lamb and Flag
11 Maiden Lane
12 Lemon Tree

Walk 4:
Holborn and Covent Garden

Distance: 2·5 miles

Route: Tottenham Court Road – Euston Road – Gower Street – Torrington Place – Tavistock Square – Tavistock Place – Marchmont Street – Bernard Street – Greville Street – Guilford Street – Doughty Street – St. John Street – Theobalds Road – Lambs Passage – Red Lion Square – Proctor Street – High Holborn – Kingsway – Gate Street – Lincoln's Inn Fields – Sardinian Street – Kingsway – Queen Street – Long Acre – Rose Street – Garrick Street – Bedford Street – Maiden Lane – Chandos Place – Bedfordbury – Strand – Charing Cross Stations.

Public Transport: Starting at Warren Street Underground Station on the Northern and Victoria Lines — Buses 10, 14, 18, 24, 27, 29, 73, 74 and 134. Finishing at Charing Cross Underground (also BR) Station on the Northern, Bakerloo and Jubilee Lines — Buses 6, 9, 15, 23 and 77A.

Refreshments: Numerous public houses, fast-food and sandwich bars.

ROUTE DIRECTIONS

Warren Street Station is on the corner of Tottenham Court Road and Euston Road. Cross the road and walk down Euston Road to Gower Street. Here on the corner, before the present roadway system was devised, stood a small tea shop (1). Walk down Gower Street and on the left hand side is University College (2), continue down Gower Street to Torrington Place, turn left, and follow the road through Tavistock Square (3), cross the roadway into Tavistock Place. At Marchmont Street turn right, and walk along Bernard Street, turn left, and almost immediately turn right into Greville Street. This leads to Guilford Street, turn left, and walk along to Doughty Street on the right hand side of the roadway. At number 48 is "Dickens House" (4). The street changes from Doughty Street to St. John Street, at the junction with Northington Street, finally reaching Theobalds Road. Cross the road, turn right, and walk along to Lambs Conduit Passage. This leads to Red Lion Square (5). On the opposite side of the square to the passage is Proctor Street leading to High Holborn. Cross the road, turn right, and walk to Holborn Underground Station on the corner of Kingsway. Opposite the station is the former Parish Church of Holy Trinity, Kingsway (6). Gate Street is the first turning on the left and here can be seen the Ship Tavern (7) the street leads to Lincoln's Inn Fields (8). Leave the Fields by way of Sardinian Street and re-enter Kingsway, turn right, and walk back towards the Underground station. Cross the road by way of the traffic lights and walk along Queen Street which leads to Long Acre. Here can be found Covent Garden Underground Station (9). Continue along the left hand side of the street to Rose Street and the Lamb and Flag public house (10). Opposite the end of Garrick Street is Bedford Street on the corner of which is Maiden Lane. Here (11) were the offices of the publishers J.M. Dent until 1972. Chandos Place leads to Bedfordbury and the Lemon Tree public house (12). From here it is a short walk to the Strand and Charing Cross Station.

POINTS OF INTEREST

1. CORNER OF GOWER STREET

The former cafe on this site was a favourite meeting place for the medical students from nearby University College Hospital. They were often joined by a bandaged male figure who disappeared when approached by the waitress. Perhaps he was the same figure who startled a guest staying at a guest house further down the road. Since the students no longer are able to call in for a quiet cup of tea and a cake due to the new roadway system he too seems to have disappeared from London's ghostly population. Where do disturbed ghosts go?

2. UNIVERSITY COLLEGE, UNIVERSITY OF LONDON

One of the Founders of University College in 1826 was Jeremy Bentham, philosopher and reformer who with a group of "lovers of religious freedom" set up a commercial company to allow non-Anglicans to receive a university education. The other, older universities, insisted that their students and staff were all members of the Established Church of England. Bentham, and others thought differently! Tradition tells that he objected to mummification although he stated in his will that he wished his body to be preserved as a permanent memorial. In one of his appearances he removed books from the shelves in the library, and has also been seen by students working late in the library. He wears white gloves and carries his walking stick the tapping of which has been heard as he walks the corridors of the college. His mummified dressed body complete with his hat is preserved in a glass case in the college. Opposite the college is the building of the University College Hospital where every new student nurse is "introduced" to Nurse Elizabeth Church. She arrived at the beginning of the twentieth century to train as a nurse and stayed to serve the hospital well, until the "fatal day" when she gave her fiance an overdose of morphine. When she died she returned in a ghostly form and has, frequently, been seen by both nurses and patients whenever the hypodermic needle is prepared for an injection of morphine.

3. TAVISTOCK PLACE AND SQUARE

A strange pair of ghosts have been seen since the mid-nineteenth century wandering around the Square and Place. One is a male figure dressed as if going to a funeral and said to have the face of a corpse under his stovepipe hat. The other is dressed either as a nanny or a nurse who approaches the man, looks at his face, screams, and runs off in the opposite direction, who, or what they are, nobody knows. Some say he is an undertaker, others suggest that he is a mourner from a recent funeral.

4. 29 DOUGHTY STREET

At number 48 Doughty Street is the house of the famous nineteenth-century novelist, Charles Dickens, and where he wrote a number of his novels. In 1971, when number 29 was being rebuilt, workmen complained that a short slim gentleman wearing dark clothes and a tallish black hat used to come and watch them at work. They finished work on the house quickly, and, according to one report left without claiming their wages. Perhaps it was Dickens being nosy or looking for material for a new book.

University College

5. RED LION SQUARE

It was common practice until late into the eighteenth century for gallows and other places of punishment to be found on the outskirts of towns and cities throughout England — and London was no exception. Fields to the North of what is now High Holborn were used for executions during the seventeenth century, and it was to Red Lion Square that the exhumed body of John Bradshaw was brought in 1661 having been removed, with that of Oliver Cromwell from their graves in Westminster Abbey. Pepys records in his Diary that in February that year the bodies of Cromwell, Ireton and Bradshaw were taken and displayed at Tyburn after they had been displayed elsewhere. All three have been seen walking around Red Lion Square over the past three hundred years and they are always in deep conversation with each other.

6. FORMER PARISH CHURCH OF HOLY TRINITY, KINGSWAY

On the site of the church, in the eighteenth century, stood a house in which the Lamb family — Charles, Mary and their mother lived. On 21st September 1796 Mary murdered her mother in a fit of temper, and having been declared insane spent some time in a mental asylum. Her mournful ghost still searches for her mother amidst the buildings on the site.

7. SHIP TAVERN, GATE STREET

The history of The Ship can be traced at least to 1549 when it was used as a secret meeting place for Catholics. As the tavern could be approached from a number of directions it was an ideal place to hold a Mass in the time of religious intolerance. A Priest would say Mass in the public bar with the congregation sitting around at tables, complete with tankards of beer!, while others were outside keeping watch for possible intruders. One priest, James Archer, who later became the Vicar General of the London District, was employed at the inn as a barman. A perfect cover! Some were not so lucky and were caught and executed in Lincoln's Inn Fields, they later returned as ghosts.

8. LINCOLN'S INN FIELDS

In addition to the Catholics from the Gate Tavern, others to be executed and to return as ghosts here include practitioners of Black Magic. Anthony Babington and his friends were executed here. The crime they were plotting was the overthrow of Elizabeth I and the restoration of the Catholic Mary Queen of Scots in her place. When arrested Babington had in his possession a wax effigy of Elizabeth I in which pins had been stuck in an attempt to procure her death by Black Magic. It is the screams of those executed here that have been heard in the quiet night hours, while an occasional dark shape has been seen lurking around the shelter in the centre of the Fields today.

9. Covent Garden Station

Jack Hayden a ticket inspector in the 1950s was making up the duty log in his office when the door handle rattled. He called out "No way here, try the stairs" thinking that a late night reveller had mistaken his office for the public toilets. The door opened and there stood a man in a grey suit and wearing a homburg hat. He turned round, and by the time that Hayden got to the door, he was walking down the spiral staircase towards the platform. He never reached it! In March 1972 he made another appearance this time to a West Indian member of the staff who promptly fainted, and put in for a transfer the next morning. Who is he? Probably William Terriss the Victorian actor who was stabbed to death outside the private door of the Adelphi Theatre in 1897. Will he return for his centenary in 1997?

10. Lamb and Flag, Rose Street, Covent Garden

If you are ever sampling the wares of The Lamb and Flag and suddenly the hanging baskets seem to start swinging, do not fear for the contents of your drink — it is only the local poltergeist making his presence known. Who "he" is nobody knows, and "his" appearances are somewhat erratic.

11. Maiden Lane

Publishers of books are not immune from visits from the "other side" as J.M. Dent and Sons Ltd. discovered during their move from Aldine House in Maiden Lane in 1972. Constant scuffling and banging was heard from the first floor of the building after staff had left for the night, and only the caretaker and his wife remained in the building. As the final removal day came nearer so the noises became more agitated. The cause of the disturbances has been attributed to a young man who had committed suicide early one evening some time before and who obviously did not approve of the publishers' departure or the future plans for the building

12. Lemon Tree Public House, Bedfordbury

In 1700 at the opening of the former Covent Garden Market the various public houses in the area were allotted a stall. The landlord of the Lemon Tree in Bedfordbury, was given one stocked with imported Italian lemons, so annoying the patriotic ghost here, who still appears from time to time and fiddles with the beer taps and throws ashtrays around the bar. Who he is nobody knows.

Kensington

1 Holland Park
2 Kensington Palace
3 Coronet Cinema
4 Ladbroke Grove
5 Cambridge Gardens
6 Chesterton Road

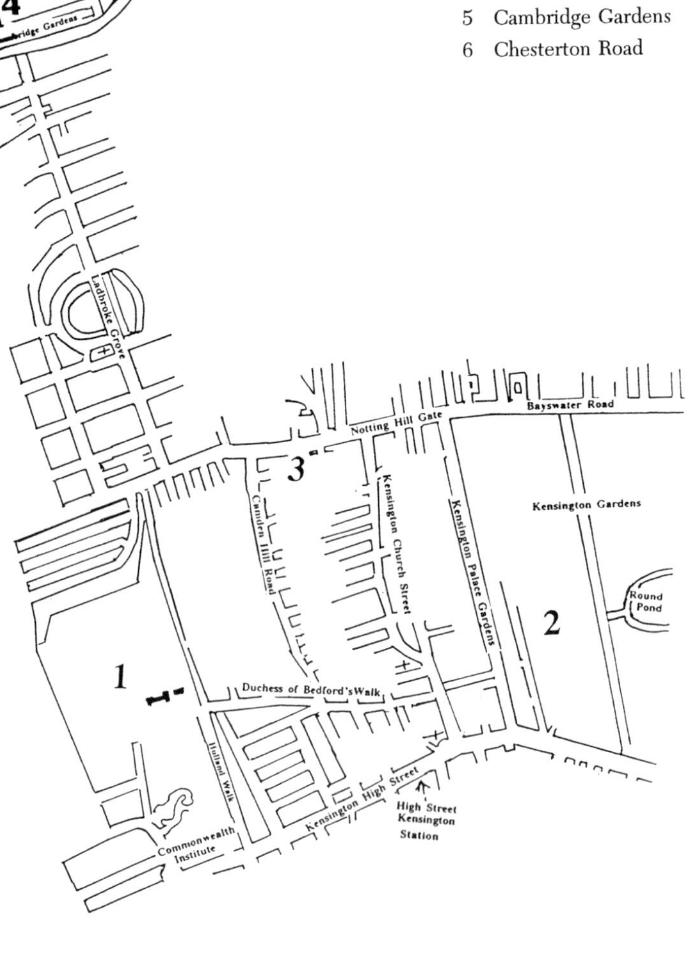

Walk 5: Kensington

Distance: 3·5 miles

Route: High Street Kensington – Holland Walk – Holland Park – Duchess of Bedford's Walk – Holland Street – Kensington Church Street – Kensington High Street – Kensington Palace Gardens – York House Place – Kensington Church Street – Notting Hill Gate – Holland Park Avenue – Ladbroke Grove – Cambridge Gardens – Oxford Gardens – Chesterton Road.

Public Transport: Starting at High Street Kensington Underground Station on the Circle and District Lines — Buses 9, 10, 27, 287, 31, 49, 52 and 70. Finishing near Ladbroke Grove Underground Station on the Hammersmith and City Line — Buses 23, 52 and 70.

Refreshments: Numerous eating places in Kensington High Street. Holland Park has its own restaurant (open-air). Notting Hill Gate has several, then there is a blank stretch until the upper parts of Ladbroke Grove.

ROUTE DIRECTIONS

At the entrance to the Underground station turn left, walk along to the traffic lights, cross the roadway, turn left and walk along to Holland Park (1). Enter the park by walking up Holland Walk that runs along the outside of the park. Immediately ahead is Holland Park House (1). Leave the park by the same gate opposite the entrance is the Duchess of Bedford's Walk that leads to Holland Road, and eventually to Kensington Church Street. Turn right and at the T-junction with Kensington High Street, cross the road. Shortly afterwards on the right hand side of the road is Kensington Palace Gardens this leads to Kensington Palace (2). To return to Kensington Church Street leave the Gardens, by way of York House Passage. To the right Kensington Church Street leads to Notting Hill Gate turn left and just past the entrance to Notting Hill Gate Underground station is the Coronet Cinema (3). Continue to walk down Notting Hill Gate and shortly afterwards when it changes its name to Holland Park Avenue, cross the roadway to Ladbroke Grove. The walk now passes through the area that is closely associated with the Notting Hill Annual Caribbean Street Festival. In earlier times there was a horse racing course here, and this is reflected in the layout of the streets. Many of them end in broad curves in keeping with the course. There are a number of eating and drinking establishments along this part of the route. At the far end of the Grove, after passing under the elevated roadway and Ladbroke Grove Underground station, there is Oxford and Cambridge Gardens (4).

POINTS OF INTEREST

1. Holland Park and House

Another ghostly visitor from the seventeenth century is a King Charles spaniel who has been seen playing on the lawn here during the daytime. Many ghosts seem to have their origins in the somewhat violent seventeenth century. Lord Holland was executed during the Civil War (1642–46) has been seen in his former London home, Holland House, now a Youth Hostel of the Youth Hostel Association (YHA), and set in the public park. The house was badly damaged in the Second World War and greatly reduced in size thereafter. Here Lord Holland would appear, preceded by three drops of blood on the floor and entering from a recess with his head in his hand in true ghostly fashion. Although his room was blitzed and not rebuilt the apparition has been seen in the hostel.

2. Kensington Palace

The figure of George II has been seen at the windows of Kensington Palace that overlook the courtyard and the weathervane on the top of the nearby building. He watches to see the change in the wind direction, waiting for news from his beloved Hanover. Sometimes he seems to wait in vain, and at other times news has come and he moves away from the windows smiling. The King lived and died here doubtless pining for his homeland.

3. CORONET CINEMA, NOTTING HILL GATE

There cannot be many ghosts with a taste for interior design apart from the one that haunts the Coronet Theatre at Notting Hill Gate. Pots of paint have been removed from a room scheduled for redecoration to one that was not, although the as yet unseen ghost has made no attempt to do the actual painting of the walls — yet.

Coronet Cinema

4. LADBROKE GROVE – CAMBRIDGE GARDENS – CHESTERTON ROAD

Anyone living in the Cambridge Gardens and Chesterton Road area of Ladbroke Grove wishing to catch a late night 'bus should take care that they do not meet the phantom 'bus that tours the neighbourhood. There was a regular service along this route, but this has long since been curtailed. People living in the area, however, have been awakened during the night by the sound of a 'bus, driverless and conductorless, without lights, hurtling through the still hours. Several motorists trying to avoid the 'bus as it rushed along its chosen route have ended their journeys in nearby hospitals with broken bones. However, it was last positively identified in 1934.

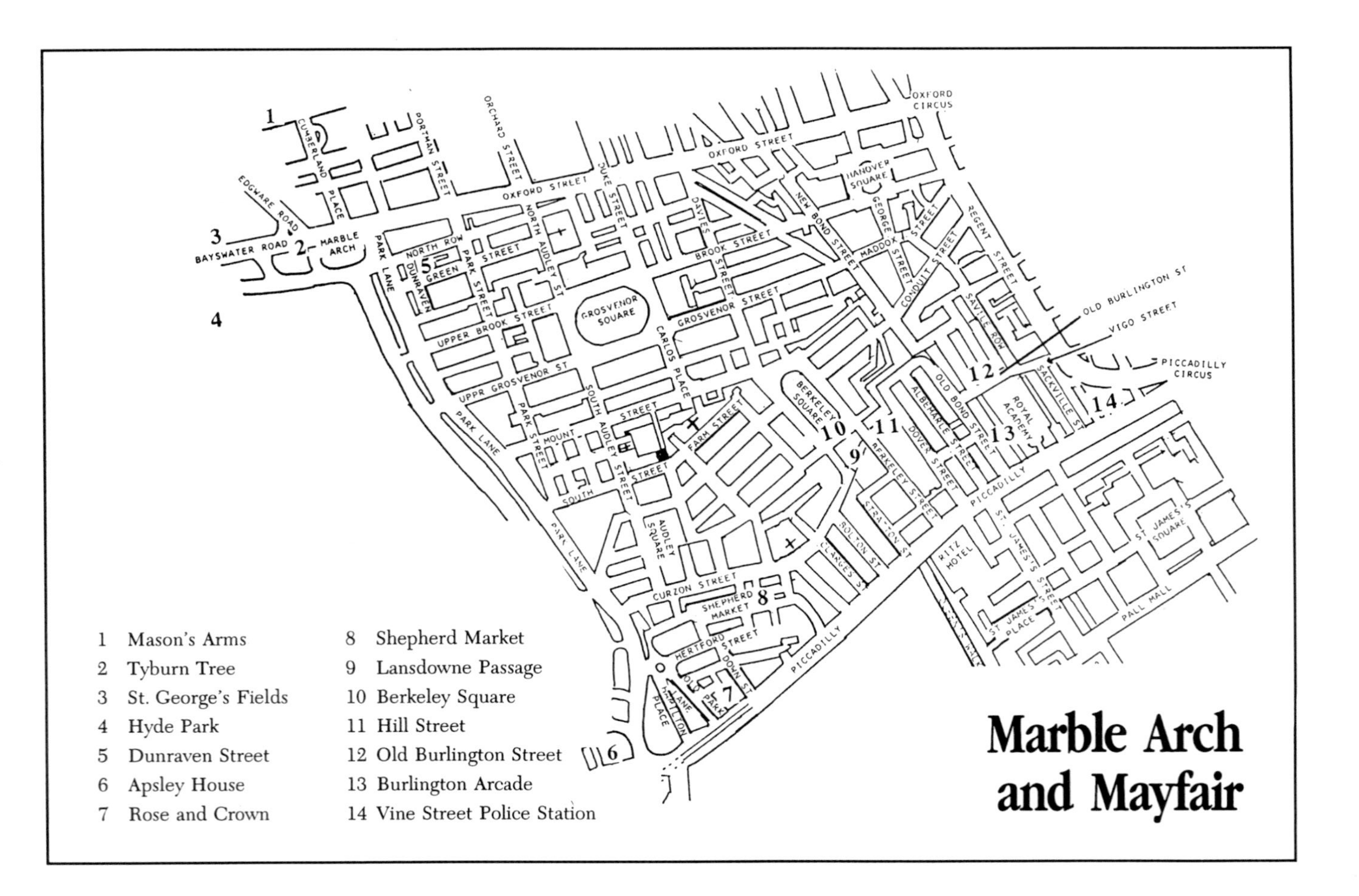
Marble Arch
and Mayfair
1 Mason's Arms
2 Tyburn Tree
3 St. George's Fields
4 Hyde Park
5 Dunraven Street
6 Apsley House
7 Rose and Crown
8 Shepherd Market
9 Lansdowne Passage
10 Berkeley Square
11 Hill Street
12 Old Burlington Street
13 Burlington Arcade
14 Vine Street Police Station
OXFORD CIRCUS
OXFORD STREET
CUMBERLAND PLACE
PORTMAN STREET
ORCHARD STREET
EDGWARE ROAD
BAYSWATER ROAD
MARBLE ARCH
PARK LANE
NORTH ROW
DUNRAVEN
GREEN
PARK STREET
NORTH AUDLEY ST
DUKE STREET
DAVIES
BROOK STREET
UPPER BROOK STREET
GROSVENOR SQUARE
GROSVENOR STREET
UPPR GROSVENOR ST
CARLOS PLACE
SOUTH AUDLEY STREET
MOUNT STREET
FARM STREET
SOUTH
HANOVER SQUARE
NEW BOND STREET
GEORGE STREET
MADDOX STREET
CONDUIT STREET
REGENT STREET
SAVILE ROW
OLD BURLINGTON ST
VIGO STREET
PICCADILLY CIRCUS
SACKVILLE ST
ROYAL ACADEMY
OLD BOND STREET
ALBEMARLE STREET
DOVER STREET
BERKELEY SQUARE
BERKELEY STREET
STRATTON ST
BOLTON ST
CLARGES ST
PICCADILLY
AUDLEY SQUARE
CURZON STREET
SHEPHERD MARKET
HERTFORD STREET
DOWN ST
OLD PARK LANE
HAMILTON PLACE
RITZ HOTEL
ST. JAMES'S STREET
ST JAMES'S PLACE
ST JAMES'S SQUARE
PALL MALL

Walk 6: Marble Arch and Mayfair

Distance: 4 miles

Route: Marble Arch Station – Cumberland Place – Upper Berkeley Street – Edgware Road – Bayswater Road – Park Lane – North Row – Dunraven Street – Park Lane – Hyde Park Corner – Old Park Lane – Shepherd Market – Lansdowne Passage – Berkeley Square – Hill Street – Old Burlington Street – Burlington Arcade – Piccadilly.

Public Transport: Starting at Marble Arch Underground Station on the Central Line — Buses 2, 6, 7, 10, 12, 15, 16, 16A, 23, 30, 36, 73, 74, 82, 94, 98, 135, 137, 137A and 274.
Finishing at Piccadilly Underground Station on the Jubilee, Bakerloo and Piccadilly Lines — Buses 3, 6, 9, 12, 13, 14, 15, 19, 22, 23, 38, 53, 88, 94, 139 and 159.

Refreshments: Limited, but there are small collections around Marble Arch and Edgware Road, and later in the vicinity of Piccadilly Circus. En route there are public houses, e.g. in Old Park Lane and in Shepherd Market.

ROUTE DIRECTIONS

Close to the Underground station at Marble Arch is Cumberland Place. Walk along the street to the third turning on the left. Here is Upper Berkeley Street (1), turn left and walk to Edgware Road, turn left. Cross over the roadway, turn left and walk back to Bayswater Road. On the road island opposite the Odeon (Marble Arch) Cinema there is a stone plaque commemorating one of the sites of the Tyburn Tree (2). A short walk away just past Stanhope Place in Hyde Park Place is the Benedictine Order of the Adorers of the Sacred Heart of Jesus of Montmartre's convent. They are an enclosed Order of Roman Catholic nuns who keep a perpetual watch before the Blessed Sacrament and pray for the repose of the souls of the martyrs of Tyburn. A few yards from the convent is an entrance to St. George's Fields (3). Opposite is Hyde Park (4). Return to the corner of Edgware Road, and by using the subways cross under the roadways to Park Lane. The first turning on the left is North Row, this leads to Dunraven Street (5). On leaving Dunraven Street return to Park Lane and walk down. Using the subway in front of the London Hilton Hotel cross under Park Lane and emerge at the Inner Carriage Way of the Park. Turn left and walk to Hyde Park Corner and Apsley House (6). Again using the subway at the corner of the house cross under Park Lane to the Inter Continental Hotel. Walk along Piccadilly to Old Park Lane (7). Return to Piccadilly and walk along to White Horse Street this leads to Shepherd Market (8). Exit from the Market, turn right, and walk along to the end of the Street. Behind the shops of today's Lansdowne Passage is a covered way (9). Curzon Street ends in Berkeley Square (10) leading from one corner of it is Berkeley Street and from here it is a short walk to Hill Street (11). Hill Street leads to Dover Street that in turn leads to Old Bond Street where on the left hand side of the roadway is Old Burlington Street (12) and finally to Burlington Arcade (13). The arcade leads to Piccadilly, turn left, and a short walk along Piccadilly is the Vine Street Police Station (14). From here Piccadilly Circus is literally "round the corner".

POINTS OF INTEREST

1. MASON'S ARMS, UPPER BERKELEY STREET

When the nearby Tyburn Tree — the most notorious gallows in London — was in full use and there was insufficient time or room on the scaffold to hang the condemned, the overflow were often housed near to the Edgware Road site. When there was room on the scaffold they were taken from where now the Masons Arms public house stands in Upper Berkeley Street to Tyburn. The cellars here are those used to house the felons, and others, and are haunted by the previous lodgers.

2. TYBURN TREE, SITE OF

Trees have played quite a significant part in the ghostly stories of the parks and open spaces in and around London, and none more so than the notorious Tyburn Tree that stood here until 1783 at the junction of the Bayswater and Edgware Roads with Oxford Street. The site is now

The site of Tyburn Tree

marked by a circular plaque on a road island at this very busy and important junction. It was one of the principal places of public hangings from the twelfth to the eighteenth century. The first permanent gallows here was erected in 1571 for the execution of John Story, "a Roman Canonical Doctor". There have been many spectacular sights at Tyburn. Highwaymen rubbing their ghostly shoulders with lovers and mistresses of the noble and royal families of the land, to saints and martyrs of the Christian Faith, both Protestant and Catholic. Among those executed at Tyburn were Perkin Warbeck the Flemish impostor and Pretender to the English Throne (1499); Elizabeth Barton, the "Maid of Kent", who denounced the marriage of Anne Boleyn to Henry VIII (1534); the last Catholic English martyr, Oliver Plunket (1681); William Dodd, a master forger (1777), Jonathan Wild, master criminal (1725). There was an estimated audience of 200, 000 present in 1750 for the hanging of James McClean. All of which makes a colourful kaleidoscope of ghostly visions.

3. St. George's Fields, Bayswater Road

Nearby, where now St. George's Fields housing estate is to be found, was one of the execution sites for deserters from the Army, a lazar hospital and a hospital for unmarried mothers. Add these together and it makes for an area rife with stories of ghostly people and scenes. One local inhabitant is recorded as saying that in 1979 whenever she looked out of her window in the vicinity of Marble Arch, she shuddered with a cold feeling creeping up her spine. On one occasion she claimed to have seen an execution taking place and that the whole area was swarming with people anxious to get a good view of the proceedings. With thousands of deaths here it is highly likely that this junction could claim to being the most haunted spot in London. Inhabitants of St. George's Fields have also reported strange happenings, with pieces of bone appearing in the window boxes and shadowy figures seen near the entrance to Bayswater Road.

4. Hyde Park

Between Marble Arch and Lancaster Gate there once stood in Hyde Park a "Devil's Elm", known locally as "Black Sally's Tree", anybody falling asleep under its branches during the night would be found dead the next morning. It was over sixty years ago that a gypsy known as Black Sally went to sleep under the tree, in spite of dire warnings from other vagrants in the park that it was an evil tree. In the morning she was dead. Since that time three other tramps have been found dead under the boughs. Although the tree was felled during the period when Dutch Elm disease was prevalent in this country, ghostly figures have been seen in the vicinity of the site that it occupied. Along this stretch of Bayswater Road a ghostly horse-bus is sometimes seen plying for hire; a reminder of the bus services here in the nineteenth century.

5. Dunraven Street, off North Row, Park Lane

Haunting number 19 Dunraven Street is no less a person than Lily Langtry, the actress, who beguiled Edward VII with her charms. The house in which she lived for a time was already haunted by other ghosts — some of the victims hanged on Tyburn Tree. A maid once met a small group of Cavalier soldiers on the stairs, while the butler saw several apparitions, their heads being carried in their hands.

6. Apsley House

The combination of Oliver Cromwell and the first Duke of Wellington, account for one of the strangest hauntings in London at Apsley House, number 1 London (Piccadilly) The appearance of Cromwell, to the Duke, who pointed to the angry crowds outside was interpreted as being a warning to him of his political activities. Cromwell has only appeared here on this one occasion.

7. Rose and Crown Public House, Old Park Lane

An alternative route from Newgate Prison to Tyburn took the criminals along Piccadilly, and Park Lane (then known as Tyburn or Tiburn Lane) to the Rose and Crown public house. This was another of the 'over-night' stopping places. Many of these unfortunates still haunt the cellars of the place that was the last place they saw before the Tyburn Tree.

Rose and Crown Public House

8. 4 Shepherd Market (formerly Sheppey's Restaurant, Mayfair)

Once an open space where the monks of Westminster Abbey held an annual fair in May (Mayfair), the area was developed in the early eighteenth century by Edward Shepherd. Described in the early nineteenth century as the Market House it was in the centre of the field known as Brook Field from the Tyburn River that flowed through it. The restaurant is the House's successor today, and although the house has long since been pulled down the restaurant has inherited some of its less desirable inmates. The cellars were once used by a notorious highwayman to store his ill-gotten gains, and as a place to rest up when he was being chased by the law officers. Tradition says that there was a tunnel from the river to the house, but it has long since been blocked up. The same story relates that another tunnel led to, or was it from, Tyburn itself. It is more likely that the latter tunnel may have connected to the Rose and Crown, Tyburn Tree being too far away. The man did however end his days suspended from Tyburn Tree but his ghost stayed behind here. He is described as being "tall, thin and dressed in a long black coat" and his favourite haunts are the bars. Cleaning ladies have often felt their dusters being pulled away from their hands. Obviously a ghost with a sense of fun!

9. Lansdowne Passage

The passage was used in earlier times as a "getaway" by the highwaymen and footpads who operated in the area in the late eighteenth and early nineteenth centuries. In spite of being built over by a shopping arcade the modern passage with bar gate at one end does not prevent the ghosts from escaping capture.

10. Berkeley Square

One of the best known and loved squares in London must be Berkeley Square in the Fashionable West End. Everybody must know the song "A Nightingale sang in Berkeley Square", but there have been happenings here of a far more gruesome nature. At number fifty it is not so much a person as a "thing", that has been described as "an oozing mess". Visitors to the house in the nineteenth century complained of seeing "it" on the floor of their rooms. It was first seen earlier in the last century at a time when the house was empty, having previously been occupied by an eccentric old man, Mr Myers, who refused to have any woman in the house. He had been jilted earlier in his life and the "thing" sent to keep females away from his house? Whatever the reason, a number of deaths are attributed to its appearances. Notes and Queries refers to the story of two sailors who spent the night in the house. One jumped from a window while the other died of fright. Lord Bulmer Lytton, the Victorian novelist, spent the night in the room armed with a revolver. This he used when the "thing" approached him, the bullet lodging in the far wall from where he was sitting. A young army officer also volunteered to spend the night in one of the rooms, and he too armed himself, and arranged to

Berkeley Square

ring a bell should he require assistance, he then settled down for his night watch. Shortly before midnight a shot was heard, and in the morning his dead body was found — he had committed suicide rather than face the "thing". There is also a supplementary story about the house concerning a young girl who dived through the window rather than submit to her uncle's advances. Yet another story tells of a young Scots girl tortured to death in the house in the last century. All of these have been seen either peering through the window of an upper storey or moving about the house. Altogether a most gruesome house. But number 50 is not the only house in the square to be haunted. At number 53 lived an attractive young lady and her father until the day she eloped with her lover, promising to return home one day. She did not keep her promise and her loving father died of a broken heart. It is his ghostly figure that can sometimes be seen standing sadly at the window of the house, dressed in a white satin coat and wearing a wig.

11. HILL STREET

The ghost of Hill Street, Mayfair is an untimely warning to those who see it that their earthly existence is about to end. Lord Lyttleton saw it in 1779 and died shortly afterwards from an unknown cause. In the eighteenth century the area in and around Berkeley Square appears to have abounded with houses where gambling went on late into the night and where houses of ill-repute could also be found. Hardly surprising, therefore, that records of the estate show constant attacks of robbery on persons coming and going from the house, having robbed their victims the assailants made good their escape through the Lansdowne Passage (9). Ghostly footsteps and hoofs have still been heard late at night in the area.

12. OLD BURLINGTON STREET

There is a flat in this street, near to the Burlington Arcade, where a violent murder took place some years ago, and anyone sleeping in the flat today is often awakened in the early hours of the morning. Visitors who do not know the macabre history of the place often refuse to spend a second night in the room where it occurred.

13. BURLINGTON ARCADE, OFF PICCADILLY

In spite of the security surrounding the Arcade there have been reports of strange "goings on" there during the hours of darkness. Known as "Percy, the Poltergeist", the ghost seems to be attracted to leather and much of his activity takes place in any shop that sells leather goods.

14. VINE STREET POLICE STATION

Not even police stations escape the haunting of former inhabitants, as the one at Vine Street bears witness. Here the ghost is that of Station Sergeant Goddard who committed suicide in one of the cells at the turn of the century. Cell doors open on their own, papers are strewn about the offices, and heavy footsteps are heard in the building.

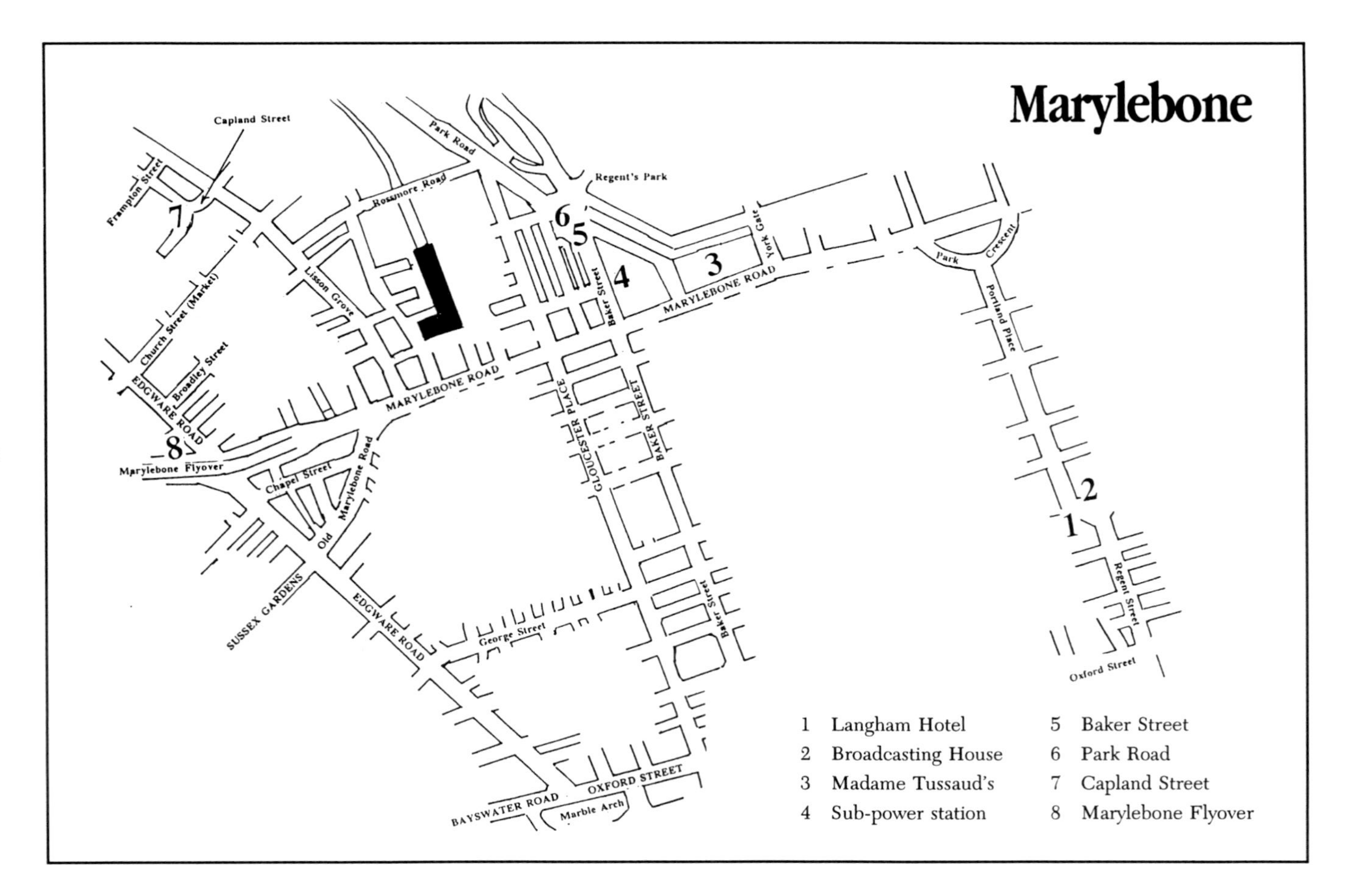

Marylebone
1 Langham Hotel
2 Broadcasting House
3 Madame Tussaud's
4 Sub-power station
5 Baker Street
6 Park Road
7 Capland Street
8 Marylebone Flyover
Capland Street
Frampton Street
Park Road
Regent's Park
Rossmore Road
Lisson Grove
Church Street (Market)
Broadley Street
EDGWARE ROAD
MARYLEBONE ROAD
Marylebone Flyover
Chapel Street
Old Marylebone Road
SUSSEX GARDENS
GLOUCESTER PLACE
BAKER STREET
Baker Street
York Gate
Park Crescent
Portland Place
Regent Street
Oxford Street
George Street
OXFORD STREET
BAYSWATER ROAD
Marble Arch

Walk 7: Marylebone

Distance: 2·5 miles

Route: Oxford Circus – Regent Street – Langham Place – Portland Place – Park Crescent – Marylebone Road – Baker Street – Park Road – Rossmore Road – Lisson Grove – Capland Street – Frampton Street – Edgware Road – Marylebone Flyover – Chapel Street.

Public Transport: Starting at Oxford Circus Underground Station on the Central, Victoria and Bakerloo Lines — Buses 3, 6, 7, 8, 12, 13, 15, 16A, 23, 25, 53, 73, 88, 94, 113, 135, 137, 139 and C2.
Finishing at Edgware Road Underground Stations on the Bakerloo (in Edgware Road), Circle, District and City & Hammersmith Lines (in Chapel Street) — Buses 6, 7, 15, 16, 16A, 18, 23, 27, 36 and 98.

Refreshments: Particularly in Baker Street, Edgware Road and Oxford Street there is a good choice of places to eat and drink. In the lesser streets an "odd pub or two" but snack bars are few and far between.

ROUTE DIRECTIONS

Exit from the Underground station by the stairs that lead to the eastern side of Regent Street and Peter Robinson's store on the corner of Oxford Street and Regent Street. The upper part of Regent Street leads to Portland Place home of the British Broadcasting Company (1) & (2). A pleasant walk along Portland Place leads to Park Crescent and Marylebone Road where on the right hand side of the roadway is Madame Tussaud's (3). Cross the roadway by way of the traffic lights opposite Tussaud's, turn left and walk along to Baker Street. Turn right, and walk past the entrance to Baker Street Underground Station. Nearby is the Lost Property Office for London Transport and at number 228 a Sub-station (4) also belonging to London Transport. Cross the roadway by way of the traffic lights and walk, past the Abbey National Building Society's offices. At the far end of Baker Street is the Volunteer public house (5). Number 7 Park Road (6) is just past the public house and the end of the road that runs along the outside of Regent's Park. Walk along the road and at Rossmore Road turn left and continue walking until Lisson Grove is reached, turn right. Capland Street (7) is the second turning on the opposite (left hand side) of the roadway. One part of the street is a cul-de-sac, following the other section to Frampton Street, turn left, and shortly Edgware Road is reached. Walk down the road to the Marylebone flyover (8). It is also possible to combine this walk with the next by taking a bus to Marble Arch.

POINTS OF INTEREST

1. Langham Hotel, Langham Place

Built on the site of Foley House, but taking its name from a later owner, the Langham Hotel was used by the British Broadcasting Company (BBC) for a number of years. It was during the "Beebe" occupation that the ghost of an Eiderdown gentleman, wearing full evening dress, was seen visiting the offices. The building has now been fully restored and is in use as an hotel once more. There have been no recent sightings of the gentleman.

2. Broadcasting House, Portland Place

Although not seen since 1937 the bewhiskered limping figure of a man at Broadcasting House was seen early one morning on the fourth floor of the building. The person who spotted him described him as having a hole in the heel of his left sock. On another occasion an engineer on his way to a studio saw a person whom he thought was a musician looking for a studio. When he drew close to the figure it disappeared. Other ghostly sightings at the House report a waiter, perhaps taking the Director General his early morning coffee.

3. Madame Tussaud's Waxworks Exhibition, Marylebone Road

The Chamber of Horrors is said to be haunted by the persons whose figures and deeds are portrayed in the chamber. In past years night watches were arranged by those interested in the supernatural but so far their findings have not been published. Today the exhibition is regularly patrolled throughout the night — but with no disturbances being entered in the log books.

4. London Transport sub-power station, Baker Street

Sarah Siddons, the famous eighteenth-century actress, lived for a short time in what today is the upper part of Baker Street, and where, earlier in this century, a sub-power station was built on the site by London Transport. The actress has been seen wandering through the "Top Gallery" which is on the site of her former bedroom. Several engineers and other members of London Transport have reported seeing her during her perambulation. She glides through walls and closed, modern, doors.

5. Volunteer Public House, Baker Street

Found sitting in an unused alcove in the cellar was the former owner of the site on which the house now stands. Rupert Nevill, whose family were Royalists during the Civil War of the seventeenth century, once farmed here, but his entire family died in a fire in one of the farm houses in 1654, now he sits and mopes in the corner. Lights in the present house, that dates from 1794, have been switched on and off without rhyme or reason, and footsteps have been heard in various places around the house which were known to be unoccupied at the time.

7 Park Road

6. 7 Park Road, Regent's Park

The smell of frying bacon or the aroma of freshly roasted coffee beans do not seem appropriate to a dental surgery. However, the one in Park Road, Regent's Park, lays claim to these ghostly smells emanating from a non existent kitchen.

7. Capland Street, off Lisson Grove, Marylebone

Said to have been murdered by their insane father three children of Capland Street make their presence known through their cries. Having lost his job, and fearing starvation for his family, the father killed himself having first murdered his entire family.

8. Marylebone Flyover, Edgware Road

The erection of a modern flyover roadway was responsible for the demolition of the Metropolitan Theatre in the Edgware Road, that traced its origins back to the White Lion public house, licensed as long ago as 1520. It had always been a place of entertainment of one kind or other throughout its long history. Gradually the performances became regular and the rooms were rebuilt as Turnham's Grand Concert Hall, It was renamed the Metropolitan Theatre in 1864 at a time when the new railway station, on the Metropolitan line brought the theatre within easy reach of lovers of the variety theatre. Here, too, as in the Coliseum in St. Martin's Lane, the ghost dated from the time of the First World War, 1914–18. It was a former theatre manager, killed during the War. He used to be seen standing at the bar at the back of the stalls, but since the flyover, opened in 1969, he has not been seen in the vicinity. Perhaps he does not like the new roadway, or the police station on the site of "his" theatre.

Soho

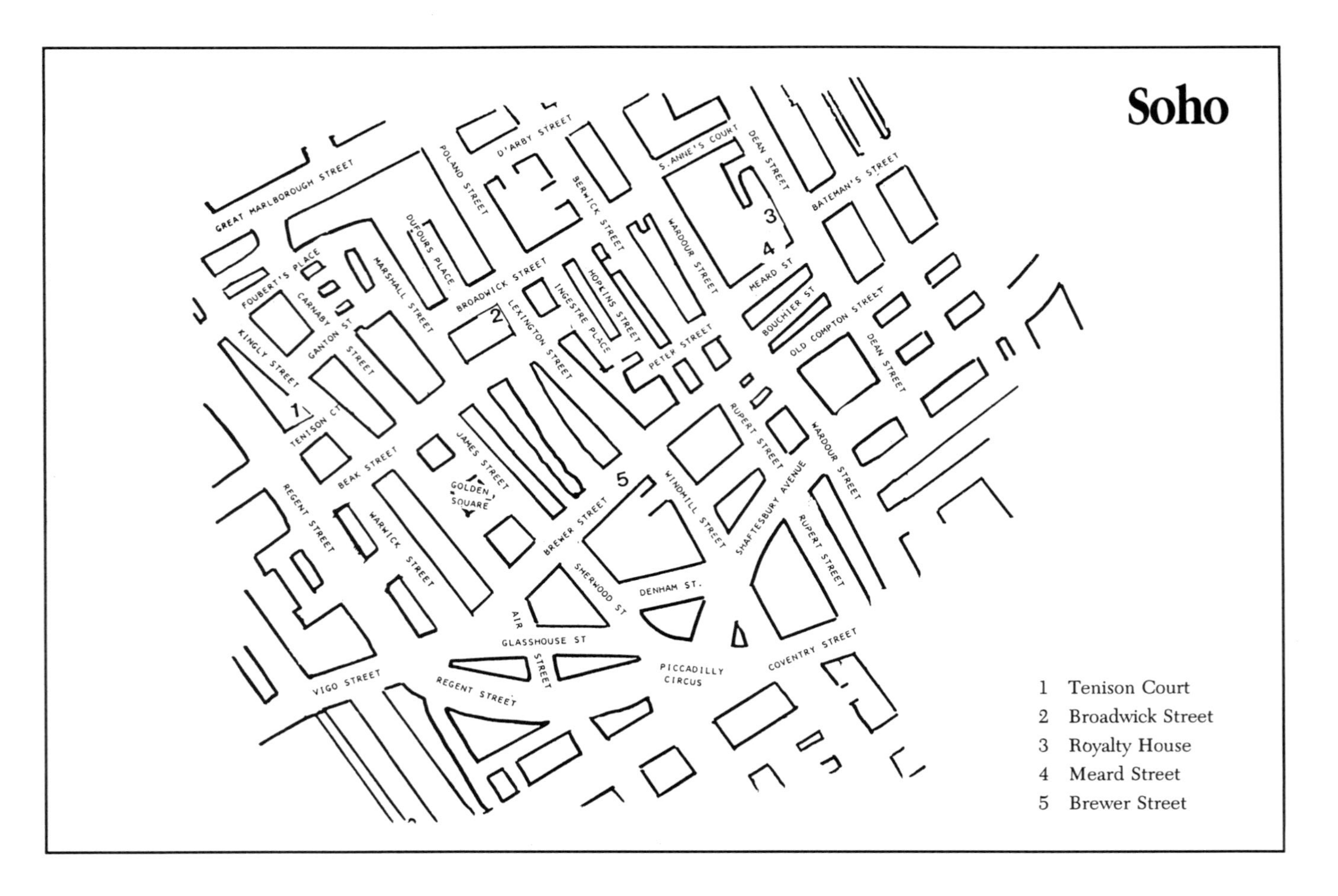

1 Tenison Court
2 Broadwick Street
3 Royalty House
4 Meard Street
5 Brewer Street

Walk 8:
Soho

Distance: 1·75 miles

Route: Piccadilly Circus – Regent Street – Tenison Court – Kingly Street – Ganton Street – Marshall Street – Broadwick Street – Wardour Street – St. Anne's Court – Dean Street – Meard Street – Wardour Street – Old Compton Street – Brewer Street – Sherwood Street – Piccadilly Circus.

Public Transport: Starting and finishing at Piccadilly Underground Station on the Bakerloo and Piccadilly Lines — Buses 3, 6, 9, 12, 13, 14, 15, 19, 22, 23, 38, 88 and 139.

Refreshments: There are a wide variety of eating and drinking places on this walk. Open seven days a week.

ROUTE DIRECTIONS

If arriving by Underground leave the station by way of the exit that leads to the east side of Regent Street. There are several 'bus stops at the same end of the street. If in doubt locate the Cafe Royal and commence the walk from there. Leave the Cafe on the right and walk along Regent Street to Tenison Court (1). At the opposite end of the Court is Kingly Street, turn left, and walk along to Ganton Street. Ganton Street leads to Marshall Street and to Broadwick Street here is the John Snow Public House (2). Continue along Broadwick Street, cross over Berwick Street and Wardour Street. Off the latter is St. Anne's Court, an interesting mix of old and new buildings. Enter Dean Street and turn right towards Royalty House (3) and shortly afterwards to Meard Street (4), again a mixture of seventeenth-century houses and later buildings. Turn left into Wardour Street and then right into Brewer Street (5). The most direct way back to Piccadilly Circus is by way of Sherwood Street. Or you may care to linger and explore the delights of Soho!

POINTS OF INTEREST

1. TENISON COURT, OFF REGENT STREET

In Tenison Court stood the church of St. Thomas, originally a chapel of ease to St. James's Church Piccadilly, and later part of the Parish of Soho. The church has now been demolished and a new secular building erected in its place. Will the ghost of a black-cassocked priest return to haunt the offices? The priest was often seen wandering around the church "deep in prayer", he would then enter the vestry at the north east corner of the church. When the verger approached him he disappeared. It is thought that he was a former rector of the parish at the turn of the century.

2. JOHN SNOW PUBLIC HOUSE, BROADWICK STREET

Not all ghosts take the form of humans as has been seen from time to time at the John Snow public house in Broadwick Street. Here the form is that of a water-pump once found nearby. The pump's handle was removed on the orders of John Snow, a doctor, during an outbreak of cholera in the early nineteenth century, in order to prevent the spread of the disease any further. In recent times a replica of the pump has been erected opposite the public house. The Phantom pump has not been seen since the replica was installed. Presumably "it" is satisfied being represented by its replacement — incidentally it does work!

The replica Phantom pump

3. ROYALTY HOUSE (THEATRE), DEAN STREET

In the heart of London's Soho is Dean Street where can be found Royalty House, built in 1834 as Mrs Kelly's Theatre and, later, renamed the Royalty Theatre. Charles Dickens acted here in the plays of Ben Jonson. The theatre has several ghosts from its rich theatrical history who still haunt the premises today. These include an old lady dressed in clothes of the nineteenth century and a lady dressed in white who walks as if going up and down stairs. The stairs have long since disappeared in the rebuilding of the former theatre. She may well have been the victim of a murder that took place here in the eighteenth century. An unknown figure also sits quietly through the performances at the theatre which has since been demolished and replaced by the present building. Finally there is the ghost of the founder of the original theatre, Fanny Kelly who, according to tradition, committed suicide here. Other ghosts such as that of a gypsy girl, murdered and then buried in a hollow wall in the old house, have been reported from time to time but may only be variations of those already mentioned.

4. MEARD STREET, OFF DEAN STREET

Built at the time of Sir Christopher Wren's birth in 1632 the house on the corner, for many years one of the most popular clubs in Soho, was haunted by Nell Gwynne the mistress of Charles II. The king bought a house for the actress in the nearby Dean Street, but when it was pulled down to make room for Royalty House Nell's ghost moved out and settled in here. One of the former owners of the club is said to have smelt her presence, there being an overpowering aroma of gardenia perfume filling the rooms wherever she entered — or could it have been orange blossom?

5. BREWER STREET

On the eve of his departure in 1798 to rejoin his ship and fight against the French in the Mediterranean Horatio, Lord Nelson is said to have visited an undertaker's shop in Brewer Street and to have ordered a coffin. His ghostly form has been seen looking towards the space where once the coffin shop stood in the middle of buildings on the south side of the street.

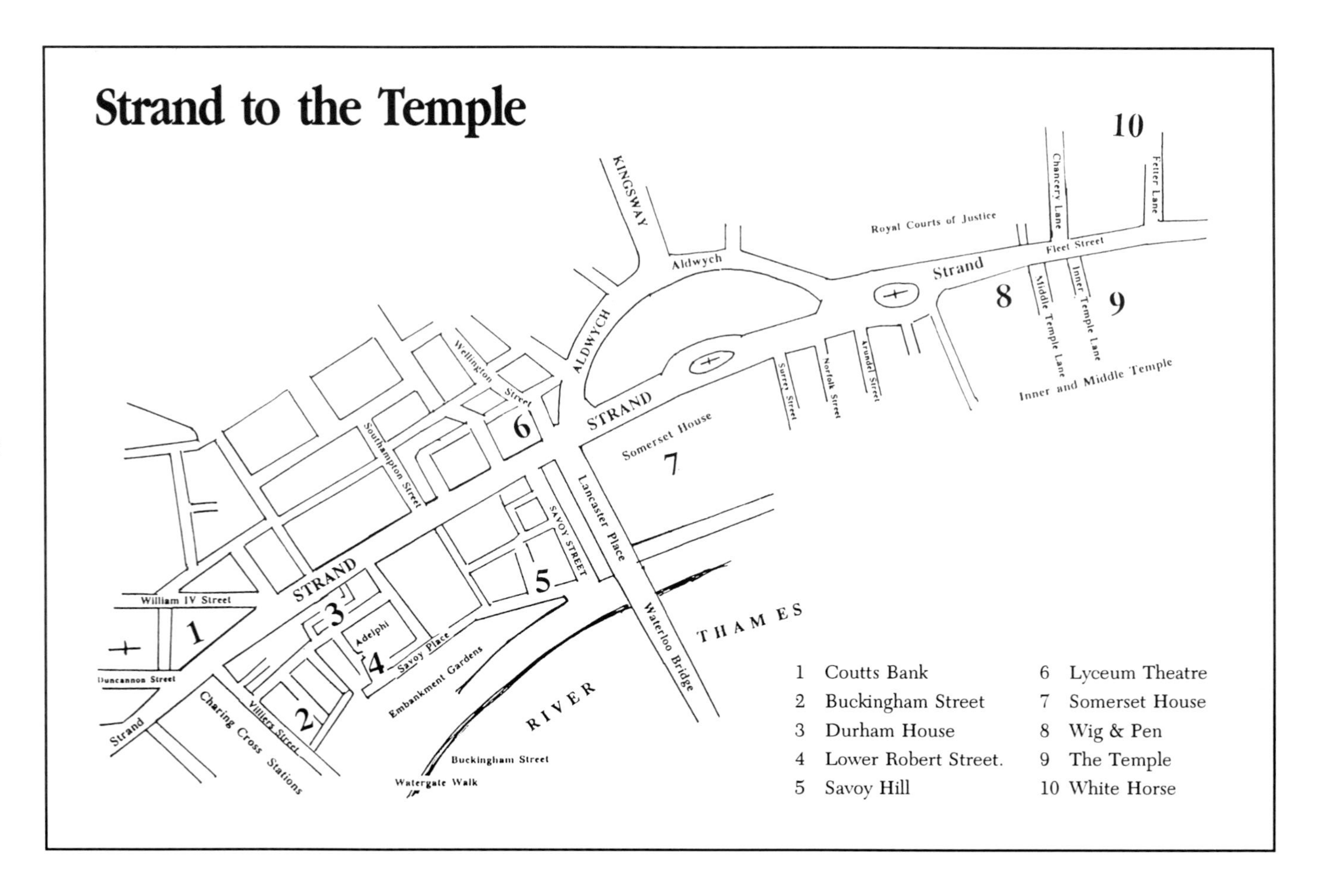
Strand to the Temple
KINGSWAY
Aldwych
ALDWYCH
Royal Courts of Justice
Chancery Lane
Fetter Lane
Fleet Street
Strand
Middle Temple Lane
Inner Temple Lane
Inner and Middle Temple
Surrey Street
Norfolk Street
Arundel Street
STRAND
Somerset House
Wellington Street
Southampton Street
SAVOY STREET
Lancaster Place
Waterloo Bridge
THAMES
RIVER
William IV Street
Duncannon Street
Strand
Charing Cross Stations
Villiers Street
Adelphi
Savoy Place
Embankment Gardens
Buckingham Street
Watergate Walk
1 Coutts Bank
2 Buckingham Street
3 Durham House
4 Lower Robert Street.
5 Savoy Hill
6 Lyceum Theatre
7 Somerset House
8 Wig & Pen
9 The Temple
10 White Horse

Walk 9: Strand to the Temple

Distance: 1·5 miles

Route: Charing Cross Stations – Strand – Villiers Street – Watergate Walk – Buckingham Street – John Adam Street – Durham Street – Robert Street – Lower Robert Street – Savoy Place – Savoy Street – Strand – Wellington Street – Strand – Temple Bar – The Temple – Fleet Street – Fetter Lane.

Public Transport: Starting at Charing Cross Underground (also BR) Station on the Northern, Jubilee and Bakerloo Lines — Buses 3, 6, 9, 11, 12, 13, 15, 23, 24, 29, 53, 77A, 88, 91, 94, 109, 139, 159 and 176.
Finishing at Fetter Lane, buses 6, 9, 11, 15 and 23 return to Charing Cross.

Refreshments: A number of fast-food and sandwich bars, plus public houses on or just off the route. Covent Garden just north of the Strand, by way of Southampton Street is "full of eating and drinking establishments".

ROUTE DIRECTIONS

Leave the forecourt of the station and diagonally opposite is Coutts Bank (1). If a closer view is required use the subway from the station forecourt to cross under the Strand, then return the same way. Along one side of the station is Villiers Street, walk down to the steps that lead to Watergate Walk. Descend the steps and walk to another short flight here is Buckingham Street (2) ascend the steps and walk along to John Adam Street, turn right, on the opposite side of the roadway is Durham House Street (3). Facing the street is Robert Street, this leads to Lower Robert Street, care should be taken in walking from one to the other. Carefully walk down the latter underneath the Adelphi buildings (4). At the end of the tunnel is Savoy Place and the back of the Embankment Gardens. Up to the time of the building of the Adelphi in the eighteenth century this was part of the river bank. Towards the end of the Place is the world famous hotel — The Savoy. The next building is the Institute of Electrical Engineers, on whose wall there is a plaque (5). Walk up Savoy Street, passing the Savoy chapel on the left to the Strand. Cross over at the traffic lights and walk up Wellington Street (6). Cross over the end of the Aldwych and return to the south side of the Strand by way of the traffic lights in front of St. Mary Le Strand Parish Church. Here is Somerset

House (7), now the home of the Courtauld Institute of Art gallery and well worth a visit! Almost at the end of the Strand is the former Wig and Pen club, now functioning as a public restaurant (8). Standing in the middle of the roadway is a tall plinth with a dragon on the top. This marks the site of Temple Bar, and a boundary of the City of London. Almost immediately on the right is the entrance to The Temple. Walk down Middle Temple Lane (9). Leave The Temple by way of Inner Temple Lane, passing under Prince Henry's Rooms, and enter Fleet Street. Cross the roadway and walk along to Fetter Lane and the White Horse public house (10)

POINTS OF INTEREST

1. COUTTS BANK, STRAND

The present Head Office of Messrs Coutts & Company the bankers occupies the site of one of the most famous shopping arcades of nineteenth century London — Lowther Arcade. By the second half of the last century the arcade had become a mecca for children at Christmas with its toys, stalls. Their ghostly apparitions still look for their choices every year at that time. During the Second World War the ghost of Baroness Burdett-Coutts was seen near her family's bank in the Strand. She was dressed in the familiar costume of the early years of this century, she has not been seen since the rebuilding of the premises. However, in 1993 the bank called upon the services of a clairsentient (someone who is able to sense spirits). He discovered a "discarnate entity" who revealed himself as an Elizabethan nobleman who claimed to have fallen foul of the Queen (Elizabeth I). The queen ordered his beheading "this took place near here" reported the ghost. The consultant then persuaded the figure to depart and never to return.

2. BUCKINGHAM STREET

It was to Buckingham Street, just behind York House's Watergate, that Samuel Pepys the diarist retired at one stage of his life, and his smiling face has been seen looking from the window on the first floor. His ghostly neighbour at number 14 is a nineteenth century painter of nudes, William Etty, with the figure seen at the upper window being probably one of his models —she looks down at the street and smiles.

3. DURHAM HOUSE, DURHAM HOUSE STREET

Durham House was the London home of the Bishop of Durham where Anne Boleyn in the sixteenth century was detained, and questioned, before being taken to the Tower of London and executed. The fine eighteenth century houses that replaced the bishops' house were demolished in 1936 to make way for the present building, but the cellars were left. Here Anne Boleyn is said to wander aimlessly around waiting for the final move to the Tower of London — and death.

4. Lower Robert Street, Adelphi

Passing through this short twisting street take care not to encounter Jenny's hole, where lives the ghost of the murdered Jenny. A poor unfortunate Victorian girl, a prostitute by trade, she was strangled by one of her dissatisfied customers and left to rot under the arches of the Adelphi. It is also said that part of the cellars here were once part of the dungeons of Durham House and are still in situ and that they occasionally make their presence known when some unfortunate victim of torture lets out a particularly nasty yell in the middle of the night.

5. Radio Station 2LO, Savoy Hill

The original home of the British Broadcasting Corporation, then 2LO, in Savoy Hill is haunted. The actress Billie Carleton, who died in the studios just after the 1918 Victory Ball had been broadcast, is said to roam the buildings. Doors to rooms, once occupied by the BBC, are said to open suddenly and people in the rooms become aware of a presence.

6. The Lyceum Theatre, Wellington Street

Madame Tussaud opened her first London Waxwork show here before taking her thirty-five wax exhibits on a country wide tour. Later she transferred them to Baker Street in 1835, and finally they moved to their present home in Marylebone Road. Could it be that the story of the lady with a man's head in her lap (told in the Theatreland Walk) was in fact Madame Tussaud with one of her exhibits?

7. Somerset House, Strand

The original Somerset House was built in the sixteenth century for the Duke of Somerset, during his time as Protector to Edward VI, but after his execution, in 1551, the house was taken over by the State and used by Elizabeth I as a residence and as a house with grace and favour apartments. Later it housed the Admiralty and during his time Horatio, Lord Nelson is said to have been a constant visitor. It is his ghost that haunts parts of the building today.

8. Former Wig and Pen Club, Strand

It is rumoured that the former Wig and Pen Club, now a public restaurant, is haunted by Oliver Cromwell whose restless body is looking for his head. Tradition says that the Lord Protector's head was stuck on a stake and rested on the top of the nearby Temple Bar. In Cromwell's day the building was in fact two early seventeenth century houses which did not become a wining and dining club until earlier in this century, originally for men of law and journalists. However, there is another ghost. An unseen man is heard whistling and walking through the rooms, usually around 2:15 in the morning. He was a solicitor in the nineteenth century found shot in his offices here.

9. THE TEMPLE

One of the more pleasing places in which to spend a really quiet time is in the Temple, sandwiched as it is between the hustle and bustle of Fleet Street to the North and the noise of London's traffic rushing along the Victoria Embankment to the South. Here is a place to "rest awhile" and soak in the peace and the history of the area. Originally the site was owned and occupied by the Knights Templars but when they were disbanded in 1312 was first given to the tenth Earl of Pembroke, then on his death in 1323 the property was given to the Knights Hospitallers. They in turned leased it to the students of Common Law. At the time of the Dissolution of the Monasteries in the sixteenth century the property reverted back to the Crown, but in 1608 James I of England (James VI of Scotland) granted the land to the Law Societies and their successors for ever. It is not at all surprising to find a ghost in the Temple. He must enjoy the peace and quiet as much, if not more than the visitors. Wearing a wig and gown he is seen from time to time by late visitors to the Temple. He has been identified as being Sir Henry Hawkins, who later became Lord Brampton. He does not disturb the peace of the Temple, simply glides from one place to another as he goes about his ghostly business.

10. WHITE HORSE PUBLIC HOUSE, 90 FETTER LANE, EC4

The last of the old City coaching houses has a ghost that wears a small dress coat and can be seen in the cellar where he rattles the bottles, after which he goes into the kitchen makes tea — but he never washes up the dirty crockery!

Middle Temple from Embankment

Theatre Royal, Haymarket

Embankment entrance to the Temple

Theatreland

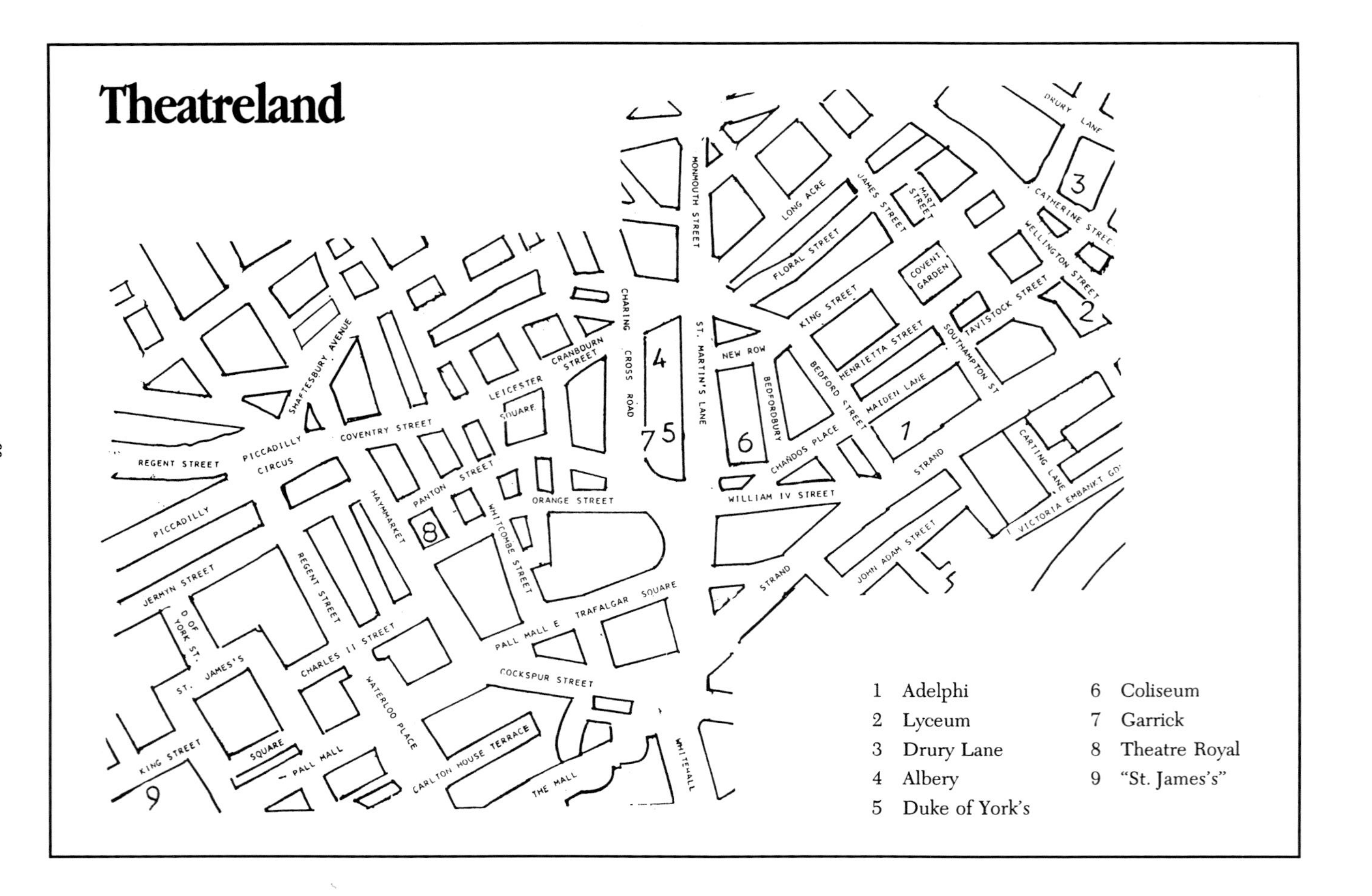

1 Adelphi
2 Lyceum
3 Drury Lane
4 Albery
5 Duke of York's
6 Coliseum
7 Garrick
8 Theatre Royal
9 "St. James's"

Walk 10: Theatreland

Distance: 1·75 miles

Route: Charing Cross Stations – Strand – Bedford Street – Maiden Lane – Tavistock Street – Wellington Street – Catherine Street – Covent Garden – King Street – New Row – St. Martin's Lane – Charing Cross Road – Irving Street – Leicester Square – Panton Street – Haymarket – Charles II Street – St. James's Square – King Street – St. James's Street – Piccadilly – Green Park Station.

Public Transport: Starting at Charing Cross Underground (also BR) Station on the Northern, Bakerloo and Jubilee Lines — Buses 1, 6, 9, 11, 13, 15, 23, 26, 76 and 77.
Finishing at Green Park Underground Station on the Jubilee, Victoria and Piccadilly Lines — Buses 8, 9, 14, 22 and 38.

Refreshments: In the Charing Cross and Covent Garden areas there are likely to be places open every day of the week. Other parts of the walk will not have quite so many open at weekends.

ROUTE DIRECTIONS

From Charing Cross Station turn right and walk along the Strand, cross the roadway at the traffic lights, turn right. At Bedford Street, turn left, and walk along to Maiden Lane here is the stage door of the Adelphi Theatre (1). Continue along the Lane to Southampton Street, cross over into Tavistock Street at the end turn right into Wellington Street and the Lyceum Theatre (2), At the foot of the street turn left along The Aldwych to Catherine Street and the Drury Lane Theatre (3). Proceed to St. Martin's Lane by way of Covent Garden and New Row. Opposite New Row is the Albery Theatre (4). Further down the lane are the Duke of York's Theatre (5) and the London Coliseum (6). At the end of the lane bear round to the right into Charing Cross Road and the Garrick Theatre (7). Proceed to the Haymarket by way of Irving Street, Leicester Square and Panton Street. The Theatre Royal Haymarket (8) is on the left of the Haymarket. Cross the street, by way of the traffic lights, and walk along Charles II Street to St. James's Square. Leave the Square by way of King Street, on the opposite side of the Square from Charles II Street this is King Street. Look on the left hand side of the road for a first floor balcony decorated with thespians (actors). Here (9) stood the St. James's Theatre. At the end of King Street (St. James's Street) turn right and walk to Piccadilly and Green Park Underground Station.

POINTS OF INTEREST

1. ADELPHI THEATRE

Since the theatrical world is so full of superstition it is hardly surprising that the theatre has more than its share of ghosts. On 16th December 1897 the newly appointed actor-manager of the, then, Royal Adelphi Theatre (Royal being dropped in 1940) William Terriss was murdered by a rival for the post — Richard Price. In true theatrical fashion Terriss took twenty minutes to die, and his last words were "Are men such fools as to believe that there is no here-after?" Since that time there have been many unexplainable happenings at the theatre — lifts work on their own, furniture is moved both on and off the stage, and it is his ghostly hand which sometimes beckons them from their dressing rooms to the stage. He is also seen at the nearby Covent Garden Underground Station as has been mentioned in a special report for London Transport.

2. Lyceum Theatre, Wellington Street

The theatre has been "dark" that is unused for a number of years. It has been haunted, in the past, by a man-like corpse that has failed identification. He disappeared completely at the time when the building was being used as a dance hall. Perhaps he couldn't stand the noise! In the last century a man and his wife were watching a performance of an opera from one of the theatre's boxes. The man's wife happened to look down into the orchestra stalls. There "sitting on the lap" of a lady member of the audience was a man's head. They tried to speak to her after the performance but lost her in the crowd. Many years later, while visiting a stately home in Yorkshire, they saw the same head in a portrait of a cavalier. On inquiring as to who the person was they were told that the family had once owned land in the Strand on which the theatre had been built. The cavalier had been beheaded at the time of Oliver Cromwell and the Commonwealth.

3. Theatre Royal Drury Lane

The "man in grey" who haunts this theatre is the only ghost working to the union rule book. Making his presence known only during the hours of 9am and 6pm, he has been seen by an increasing number of people, members of the acting profession as well as the general public. On one occasion he entered a room containing over one hundred people, all of whom later claimed to have seen him. He is considered to be a good critic and if seen during the early stages of production it is taken to be an omen of success for the show. Proof of this in recent years have been the number of musical shows that he has patronised. All the shows were a brilliant success and include "The King and I", "South Pacific", "Oklahoma", "Carousel" and more recently "Chorus Line" and "Miss Saigon". During the run of Ivor Novello's "Dancing Years he was seen by both actors and audience — but only during the matinee performances. Several up and coming actresses claim to have been helped by this ghost. One actress felt her skirt being tugged to change her position on the stage, with a result that the audience laughed more readily. So impressed was she that she kept her new position for the remainder of the production. If rumour is to be believed then the ghost is Arnold Woodruff, who was killed in a fit of anger by actor-manager Charles Macklin some two hundred years ago. Those who have seen him say that he is dressed in the costume of the eighteenth century. During the rebuilding of the theatre in the last century workmen found a skeleton of a man bricked up in one of the walls — a dagger in his ribs. There are two other ghosts at the theatre, both of whom were dearly loved by audiences in the past. One is perhaps the most famous clown of all time — Joe Grimaldi; and the other Dan Leon a great comedian, who once came face to face with Stanley Lupino. Opposite the theatre is the Opera Tavern where the ghost of a man found murdered here attracted the attention to the place where his body had been buried by the rattling of bottles in the cellar.

4. ALBERY THEATRE, ST. MARTIN'S LANE

Built originally in 1903 on a plot of spare land after the building of another theatre, Wyndhams, in Charing Cross Road, Charles Wyndhams erected the New Theatre, now renamed Albery Theatre. It is his ghost which has been seen in the theatre when the building is empty of an audience and only security staff are on duty, or, on stage, particularly during rehearsals when he gives his ghostly approval, or otherwise, to the actors.

5. DUKE OF YORK'S THEATRE, ST. MARTIN'S LANE

Opening as the Trafalgar Theatre in 1892 but renamed the Duke of York's in 1895 the theatre does not have one "resident ghost" but several. There have also been a number of unexplained happenings over the years that can only be attributed to the supernatural. One of the props used during a 1940s production of a play about Queen Victoria was an old bolero-style jacket. Whoever wore it complained of the most unpleasant sensation, as though the garment was shrinking on her body. On another occasion it nearly strangled the actress wearing it. Several other actresses wore the jacket with the same effect. It was later sold to an American collector of Victorian clothing, and when his wife tried it on she became exceedingly distressed and would not wear it agáin. Its present whereabouts are unknown. In the "Royal Room", a place set aside for the entertaining of distinguished visitors, the ghost of the eccentric wife of the first manager — Frank Wyatt — makes occasional visits. However, she does not confine her appearances to this room, but has also been seen mingling with the audience. Other strange phenomena include a flying coffee pot and keys that drop down from nowhere.

6. LONDON COLISEUM THEATRE, ST. MARTIN'S LANE

The London home of the English National Opera company, the Coliseum was built originally by Sir Oswald Stoll, as a variety theatre. Its ghost is from neither the world of opera nor variety, but is the ghost of a soldier from the First World War, 1914–18. The story is that he spent his last night of leave at the theatre, and on returning to the Front, was killed. He wanders round the Circle looking for his seat. The date of his death 3rd October 1918, is the first recorded date of his appearance.

7. GARRICK THEATRE, CHARING CROSS ROAD

At the time of a recent refurbishing of the theatre there was some concern as to whether it might disturb the ghost, believed to be that of a former manager of the theatre in 1915 — Arthur Bouchier. He is said to haunt the upper parts of the building — the "gods". During the time of the work he was seen by several of the workmen, and others working on the stage. The theatre was built for W.S. Gilbert in 1889 and stands over the underground River Cranbourne. Scandal hit the theatre at the end of the nineteenth century when Mrs Ebbsmith was found in the

River Thames with a ticket stub from the Garrick in her hand. At the time a play "The Notorious Mrs Ebbsmith", by Sir Arthur Pinero, was being performed at the theatre. She too has been seen in the building.

8. THEATRE ROYAL, HAYMARKET

One ghost that all actors are only too pleased to see is that of John Baldwin Buckstone at the Theatre Royal Haymarket. Opening as the Little Theatre in 1720, it changed its name in 1766 to become the Theatre Royal in the Haymarket, and, finally, in 1885 the Theatre Royal Haymarket. In 1853 John Buckstone arrived, as its new manager, and has remained there ever since! When he died in 1878, his ghost stayed on to welcome, or otherwise, players and their plays. He has been heard rehearsing his lines, and on one occasion the actor Victor Leslie discovered him in his dressing room. Thinking that he was an intruder he promptly locked the door and sent for the police, who, on arrival found the locked room empty. On another occasion he actually appeared during the performance of "At the drop of a Hat" standing behind Michael Flanders, and was seen by several members of the audience. His appearance is said to be forecast of a good long run by the current production.

9. ST. JAMES'S THEATRE, KING STREET (FORMER SITE OF)

One theatre that has long since disappeared was St. James's Theatre in King Street, opened in 1835 and used by Charles Dickens for the production of his operatic burlesques. But the ghosts here were not strictly theatrical ones but persons who had lived in a house on the site in the eighteenth century. They were dressed in the costumes of the day. There have been no recorded sightings since offices were built on the site of the former theatre.

Westminster

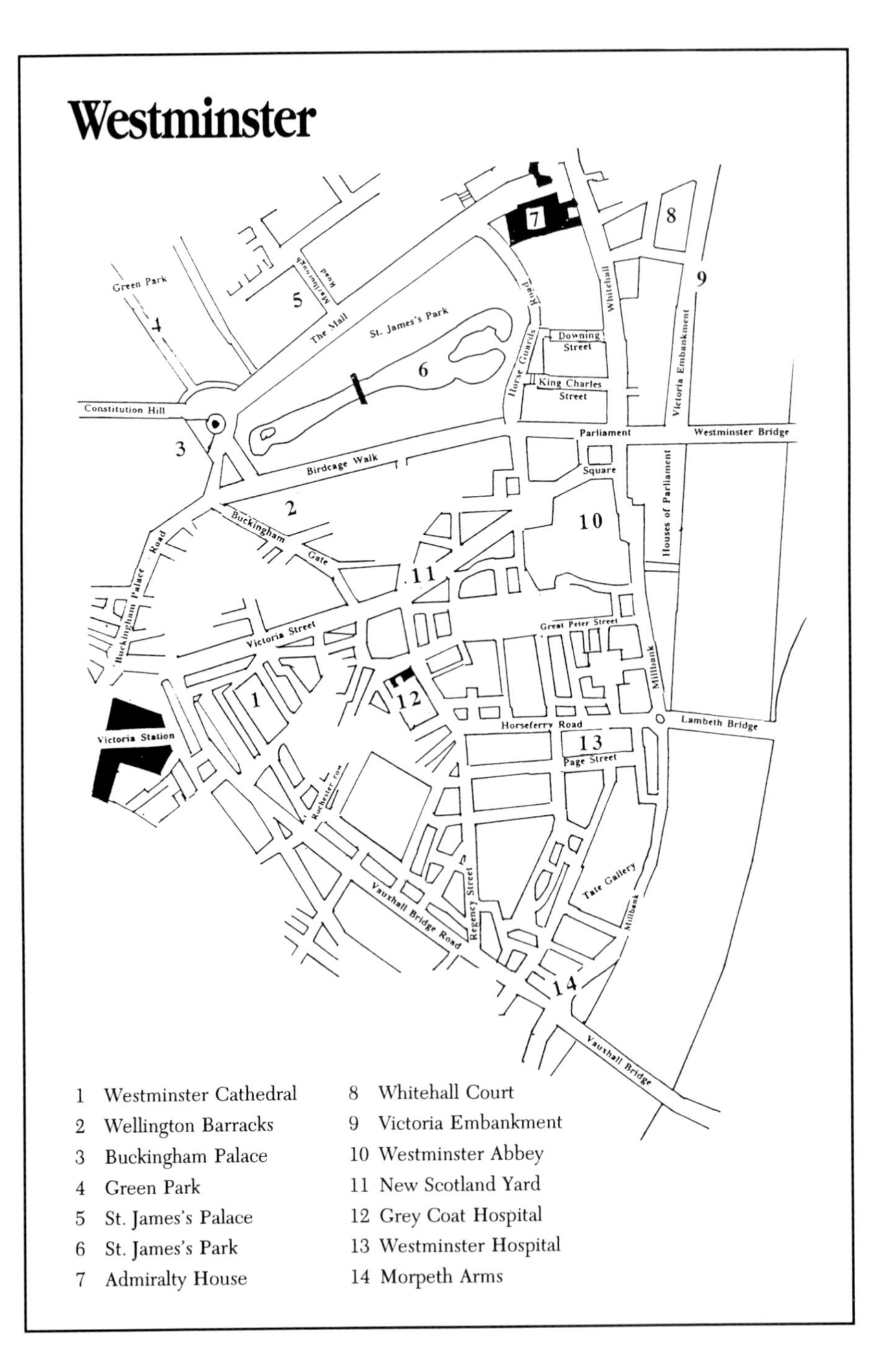

Walk 11: Westminster

Distance: 5 miles

Route: Victoria Station – Victoria Street – Cathedral Piazza – Westminster Cathedral – Victoria Street – Buckingham Gate – Birdcage Walk – Buckingham Palace – Constitution Hill – Green Park – The Mall – St. James's Park – Horse Guards Road – The Mall – Admiralty Arch – Whitehall – Admiralty House – Whitehall Place – Whitehall Court – Horse Guards Avenue – Victoria Embankment – Bridge Street – Parliament Square – Westminster Abbey – Victoria Street – Strutton Ground – Grey Coat Place – Horseferry Road – Millbank – Vauxhall Bridge.

Public Transport: Starting at Victoria Underground (also BR) Station on the Circle, Victoria and District Lines — Buses 2, 8, 9, 11, 16, 24, 36, 38, 52, 73, 185, 211 249, 319, 507, C1 and C10.
Finishing at Pimlico Underground Station on the Victoria Line — Buses 2, 36, 77A, 88, 185 and C10.

Refreshments: Plenty in the Victoria area, a few scattered ones on the rest of the route.

ROUTE DIRECTIONS

The walk is best started from "Little Ben" clock tower at the end of Vauxhall Bridge Road, at the junction with Victoria Street. Cross the road island on which the clock stands and walk along Victoria Street to the Cathedral Piazza (1). Return to the piazza, turn right, cross the roadway, at the traffic lights. Walk to the right, past the City of Westminster Council's offices to Buckingham Gate, turn left and walk along to the end of the road. Turn right into Birdcage Walk and the Wellington Barracks (2). Using the traffic lights cross the roadway to the corner of St. James's Park, walk along Spur Road cross over the road to the pedestrian precinct in front of Buckingham Palace (3). To the right is Constitution Hill, cross by the crossing to Green Park (4). Enter The Mall, on the left hand side of the roadway and walk along to St. James's Palace (5). Return to The Mall, cross over to St. James's Park (6). Walk through the park to Horse Guards Road, turn left and return once more to The Mall. Turn right, pass under Admiralty Arch, and walk into the top end of Whitehall. Here is the former Admiralty House (7), Cross Whitehall and walk down Whitehall Place to Whitehall Court (8), Follow the court to the end and turn left along Horse Guards Avenue. This leads to the Victoria Embankment and the River Thames (9). At the junction of Victoria Embankment and Westminster Bridge cross the roadway to Bridge Street. Walk away from the bridge to Parliament Square and Westminster Abbey (10). The end of Victoria Street is opposite the West Front of the Abbey, walk along on the right hand side to New Scotland Yard. (11). Opposite "The Yard" is Strutton Ground, a good outdoor market, this leads to the Greycoat Hospital (12). Follow the roadway to the left hand side of the school — Horseferry Road. Here, on the right, is the former Westminster Hospital (13). At the end of the road is Millbank, turn right, and walk past the Tate Gallery to the Morpeth Arms (14).

POINTS OF INTEREST

1. Westminster (Roman Catholic) Cathedral

A sacristan, the person responsible for the altar and sacred vessels used in church divine services, saw a black-robed figure near the high altar of Westminster Cathedral in Victoria. Although the present building only dates from the latter half of the last century in Pre-Reformation times the site was owned by Westminster Abbey. During the wars with Scotland and the Civil War of the seventeenth century a prisoner of war camp was set up on the site with black-robed chaplains attending the spiritual needs of the prisoners. The figure seen by the sacristan walked away into the night when approached, and a thorough search of the building failed to find any possible intruder. The cathedral authorities have always refused to confirm or deny the presence of this ghostly "one man congregation", but the story persists. There is little doubt in some people's minds that the ghost exists and that he is a visitor from the past history of the site of the present cathedral.

2. Wellington Barracks, Birdcage Walk

The chaplain and his wife had been entertaining friends to dinner. After the guests had left the wife started clearing the dining room table and began the washing up. Meanwhile her husband was seeing their friends off from the car park. As she stood at the kitchen sink a shadow past over her. Thinking that it was her husband she said "You're back quick from seeing them off". There was no reply as the door of the kitchen shut with a slight bang. Several minutes later the chaplain put his head around the door and said "I'm back now dear. They had trouble starting their car and I had to go to the Motor Pool for help". "You came into the room a few minutes ago didn't you?" "No" he replied, "I have been away for at least fifteen minutes". "Who came in then?" asked his wife. They never did find out!

3. Buckingham Palace

Two ghosts have been recorded in and around Buckingham Palace. The first is a black-robed monk who is said to have been imprisoned here in medieval days when the land was owned by Westminster Abbey. This being close to where now Westminster Cathedral stands, that is on the site of an annual fair, could he have been caught in an improper situation for a monk and so was punished? A private secretary to Edward VII once saw a ghostly figure resembling Nell Gwynne who was very familiar with the Mulberry Pleasure Gardens that once stood here. Samuel Pepys records in his diary a visit to the Gardens, and seeing Nell Gwynne there. She appears never to have left the place!

4. Green Park

A place to avoid if you are frightened of ghosts! There in the early hours of the morning has been heard the clashing of steel as two unseen figures fight a duel. At other times, through the early morning mists can be heard the cries of the nuns from the nearby Lazar House who were turned out of their rooms by Henry VIII, who wanted to use their refectory for a feast that he had planned. Happening as it did in the middle of winter, many of the nuns died from frost bite and the bitter cold, and it is their cries which penetrate the early morning mists. It is also, according to legend, why no flowers grow in the area; hence the name Green Park. To this should be added the fact that the Tyburn River still flows under the park, and this, in former days, caused the area to be a morass rather than pleasant flower growing fields. Within the park is the Tree of Death, so named because of the number of suicides committed there. Park wardens have reported that a noise comes from the tree to the surprise of passers-by, and children have been known to avoid playing in the immediate vicinity. A tall dark figure has also been seen under the tree, but a second glance shows that he has disappeared — into the tree.

5. St. James's Palace

The ghostly apparition is no respecter of class, race or religion and the Royal Family and their friends have been associated with them over the years. On the site of a twelfth-century foundation Lazar (Isolation) Hospital, Henry VIII had built for himself a new and splendid palace of St. James (the Less), in the sixteenth century, retaining the dedication of the hospital. In this royal residence that has seen much of the history of England in good and bad times, there are two or three particular ghosts to rout out from their hiding places. The first is that of the Duke of Cumberland's valet, an Italian named Sellis, discovered one morning with his throat slit 'from ear to ear'. It is said that the valet committed suicide having discovered that the Duke, son of George II, had seduced his daughter. How he slit his own throat is not known as no weapon was ever found in the room. It seems more likely that the Duke, in a fit of temper, killed his servant because of

St. James's Palace

the discovery. After the event the Duke was seldom seen in public again in England, and when he was he was booed by the crowd. Two ghosts were French ladies, friends of Charles II. One, the Duchess of Mazarin was mistress to Charles II, and the other Madame de Beauclair, mistress to James II. They made a promise to each other that who ever died first would return in spirit form to visit the other from time to time. The first to die was Madame de Beauclair who duly appeared to her friend the Duchess. Although the latter was healthy, she said that she would like to join her friend and quite suddenly, at midnight she died. Now they wander around the palace looking for the rooms that they know so well. Since their deaths in the seventeenth century there has been a disastrous fire and little remains of the actual palace of Henry VIII that they knew.

6. ST. JAMES'S PARK

How many of the thousands of people who stroll through, have their lunch, or feed the fowl in St. James's Park would return in the evening, on their own? A soldier returning to his billet earlier than expected one evening found his wife in the arms of another soldier, whereupon he stabbed her and struck off her head.

He buried her body in the park and her head in the barracks grounds, and now the ghost of a headless woman is said to rise from the water of the lake, terrifying late night visitors to the park as she runs across the grass in search of her head. Soldiers on guard duty in nearby Wellington Barracks have seen her in the past, and in 1804 her presence was quoted in a court of law. A motorist, driving down The Mall late one night in 1972, swerved to avoid hitting a woman dressed in red about to cross the road in front of him. He left the road and hit a lamp-post although perfectly sober at the time. The story of the haunting was told in court and the driver was acquitted.

7. ADMIRALTY BUILDING, WHITEHALL

Standing at one end of Whitehall is the building built by Thomas Ripley between 1722 and 1726, and later enlarged to become Admiralty House, the official residence of the First Lord of the Admiralty. The ghost of the house is Margaret Reay, mistress of the Earl of Sandwich, Lord Commissioner of the Admiralty who, on 7th April 1779, was shot dead by the Reverend James Hackman, a jealous lover, when leaving Covent Garden Theatre. When Denis Healey was Defence Secretary in 1969 newspapers reported the ghost of the house being active.

8. NATIONAL LIBERAL CLUB, WHITEHALL COURT

A supernormal happening but hardly a ghost used to be heard at the National Liberal Club, near Whitehall which stopped when a young German girl who was employed by the club as a maid was dismissed from the job. During her employment strange noises were often heard apparently surrounding her wherever she went about the premises. No member of the staff could account for this strange phenomena. But when she left so did the noises.

9. VICTORIA EMBANKMENT

Stretching from Blackfriars Bridge in the City of London, all along the river bank to Westminster Bridge is the Victoria Embankment. Constructed between 1862 and 1874, it was the work of Sir Joseph Bazalgette. Situated on the Embankment is Cleopatra's Needle, erected in Egypt in 1500BC and brought to London in 1877. The spot used to be a favourite place for suicides and for would-be suicides. In turn, some of the former have returned in ghostly form to the site of their watery demise. However, when they are approached they disappear from the sight of would-be rescuers. A policeman, in 1920, was approached late one night, by a highly excited young girl who was speechless but gesticulating towards the river where another girl was about to jump into the river. He looked towards the second girl but when he turned back to the first he discovered that she had disappeared. And, turning back once more towards the second girl found that she had disappeared as well!

10. WESTMINSTER ABBEY

Westminster Abbey was built on a site in Roman times that saw the dedication of a temple to Apollo. This was possibly consecrated as a Christian church before being rebuilt, c.616, during the reign of King Sebert who himself lies buried in the abbey's south choir aisle. During various rebuildings the level of the floor has changed considerably which may account for one of the ghosts of the Abbey, a black-robed Benedictine monk, appearing to float above the present floor level. He is heard talking to himself long before he is seen going about his ghostly way. He lost his life near the high altar having pursued a gang of thieves from the nearby Sanctuary, through the church. Since the time of Elizabeth I the Abbey has been in charge of the Dean and Chapter. During the seventeenth century the President of the Court set up to judge Charles I, used the Deanery as a house, and here, in January 1649 signed the King's death warrant. His restless ghost still haunts the chamber where he signed the fatal document. More recently these historic ghosts have been joined by a modern one — the Unknown Warrior near the west door of the Abbey. A verger on late night duty a few years ago saw a soldier standing looking down at the tomb, and on reporting the matter in the morning was told that others had also seen the figure. Some say it is his brother or a fellow soldier of the first World War, who keeps a lonely watch here. In the twelfth century the Abbey set up a cell abbey at Hurley, near Maidenhead, which was founded, as was the present Westminster Abbey by Edward the Confessor and his sister, Editha. On her death she asked to be buried at Hurley, and when some sixty years ago excavations were taking place at Hurley the "Grey Lady" was seen. Colonel Rivers-Moore who owned the house on the site of part of the abbey failed to find her tomb, and when the digging ceased so did the appearance of the "Grey Lady".

11. NEW SCOTLAND YARD, VICTORIA STREET

When the Metropolitan Police moved their headquarters, together with the famous Black museum from the Embankment near Westminster Bridge to Victoria Street, all hoped that the ghost of a nun, her face covered with a veil, would stay behind. She did not, preferring apparently to remain with the gruesome items in the museum, and has been seen keeping solitary watch over the exhibits. The museum is not open to the general public.

12. GREY COAT HOSPITAL (SCHOOL)

In the late seventeenth century a number of charity schools were founded in London and each of them was distinguished by the colour of their uniforms. One such school was the "Royal Foundation of Queen Anne in the Parish of Saint Margaret's, Westminster, commonly called "The Grey Coat Hospital", it still flourishes today. Its ghost however dates from the following century when an apprentice from Christ's Hospital murdered the nurse (matron) to the hospital

Mrs Martin. He made his escape through the window of her room —now a staff room. At one time her ghost used to walk the boys' dormitory, when it was a mixed school, this is now the Music Room. Pupils in the present century have been known to avoid the gallery of the hall saying that her ghost haunts there too.

13. WESTMINSTER HOSPITAL, DEAN RYLE STREET

Nursing staff of this former hospital reported on several occasions a sighting of the "Grey Lady" who visited various wards there from time to time. Her appearance often foreboded ill for the occupant of the bed she visited which caused her to be known as the "Angel of Death". Nobody seemed to know who she was or from where she came. Perhaps she was a nurse to the prisoners who were once imprisoned here during the Civil War of the seventeenth century.

14. MORPETH ARMS PUBLIC HOUSE, MILLBANK

Before the building of the Embankment in the nineteenth century Millbank housed the notorious Millbank Penitentiary where prisoners who had been sentenced to transportation to the Colonies were kept prior to being herded aboard barges in the Thames to take them to the ships, anchored in the Upper Pool of London, that would transport them to the southern hemisphere. The cellars of the Morpeth Arms, Millbank, are connected to a tunnel through which the prisoners were taken in order that they might not be given the chance to escape, or be rescued by their friends. A ghostly hand taps the shoulder of any unwary person who lingers too long in the cellars and water drips on their head, from an apparently dry vault.

Buckingham Palace

Walk 12:
Oddspots

Throughout London there are a number of "Odd Spots" that have ghostly overtones. Here is a small selection, some of which form a small group that can easily be visited from nearby Underground railway stations.

BELGRAVIA

EATON PLACE

(Nearest Underground station: Victoria)

At the precise moment on the 22nd June 1893 when Admiral Sir George Tryon's flagship, H.M.S. Victoria, collided in the Mediterranean with Admiral Markham's H.M.S. Camperdown, Sir George, in complete naval uniform, appeared at an "At Home" being given by his wife at their house in Eaton Place.

WILTON ROW, OFF WILTON CRESCENT

(Nearest Underground station: Hyde Park Corner)

A party of officers from the nearby Knightsbridge Barracks were playing cards one evening in the early nineteenth century at the Grenadier public house here, when one of them was found to be cheating. The rest of the party took him outside and resulting from a combination of anger and drink, flogged him to within one inch of his life, then left him and returned to the card playing inside the house. The officer staggered down the steps in front of the house, where he died. He is seen, usually in September, the month of his death, on the steps of the house, or, occasionally inside the building quietly standing at the foot of a bed.

GREENWICH

QUEENS' HOUSE

(Nearest BR station: Greenwich)

The Queens' House, designed by Inigo Jones one of the earliest Palladian style buildings in England, has a photogenic ghost. Two Canadians visiting the house in 1960 took photographs of the tulip staircase which leads from the foyer to the upper rooms of the house. When their photographs were developed, the prints showed what appeared to be two female figures chasing each other up the stairs. Photographs taken since have failed to reveal any further evidence of the haunting.

ROYAL NAVAL COLLEGE

Across the road from the Queens' House, and standing on the site of a former royal palace, is the former Royal Naval Staff College soon to move to Camberley, in Surrey. It was here that Admiral Byng in 1757 was detained following his trial for treason, of which he was found guilty. After his execution on board the Monarque in March the same year his ghost was seen in the Queen Anne building of the college, and since that time mysterious footsteps have been heard, and a figure in a shroud (burial garment) has been seen, both of which have been associated with the Admiral.

BLACKHEATH

On the far side of Greenwich Park is Blackheath in former times a lonely spot that was infested with highwaymen. Here came English kings, fresh from victory in France, and here, too, gathered rebels like Wat Tyler in 1381, protesting against the imposition of a Poll Tax. The first English golf club was founded here in 1608, as the Society of Golfers, which had the royal seal of approval of James I of England (James VI of Scotland). But it is not the ghost of a golfer which is sometimes seen on the heath on quiet autumn evenings. Rising from the mist there appears a shadowy figure of a woman attired in dark Victorian garb. She came here to keep a clandestine appointment with her lover. He failed to arrive and in desperation she hanged herself from a nearby tree. The last sighting was in 1970.

HAMPSTEAD

HEATH STREET, WILLIAM IV PUBLIC HOUSE

(Nearest Underground station: Hampstead)

After a visit to the dentist in Heath Street a young girl committed suicide there but her ghost has only been seen at the window of the William IV public house.

HAMPSTEAD HEATH

(Nearest Underground station: Hampstead)

Dick Turpin, the most famous highwayman of all times, has been seen a dozen times or more riding Black Bess across the Heath. He gallops the Vale of Health towards the Spaniards Inn where he used to hide his horse in a cellar. Tunnels under the building enabled Turpin to escape the Bow Street Runners when they chased him. Presumably the Runners were delayed by the landlord of the inn with a drink or two while Turpin rode away to safety. Over the years a number of landlords have heard the thumping of hoof beats but on investigation found nothing more sinister than a door which had not been properly closed.

Dick Turpin is not the only ghostly robber to be seen on the heath. Others have been seen there too; but perhaps they were warned of the approach by humans by a stone that whistles in the night at the place where one of the

highwaymen met his end — on a noose. Born at Kingston-upon-Thames, in Surrey, Jerry Abershaw became one of the most daring highwaymen of the eighteenth century.

ADAMSON ROAD

(Nearest Underground station: Swiss Cottage)

In a basement flat here there once appeared a deformed dwarf, hiding in a child's toy cupboard. He became known as "Little Charley" and his presence was often heralded by the movement about the room of knives and forks, scissors, and even on one visit a plate of fish and chips. When the tenancy of the flat changed he was never seen or heard of again.

HIGHGATE

HIGHGATE CEMETERIES — OLD AND NEW

(Nearest Underground station: Archway or Highgate)

Over 50,000 bodies lie buried within the new and old Highgate cemeteries which date from the early nineteenth century, and there are constant sightings of supernatural phenomena. When they were left neglected and derelict the two sites were often the subject of ghostlike vampire sightings, particularly in the 1970s when Allan Farrant a "self-styled vampire hunter" was very active. The local newspapers of North London in 1970 carried several reports of Black Magic rites here and the cemeteries acquired a reputation of evil repute following the desecration of some of the vaults. Described as being one of the "spookiest places in London", it does have its fair share of ghosts including an old woman seen wandering through the tombstones looking for the place where her murdered children are buried, and the ghost which peered through the railings at a motorist whose car had broken down. Needless to say, the motorist did not wait to find out the reason for the apparent breakdown, but promptly fled the spot.

OLD GATE HOUSE PUBLIC HOUSE

In the fourteenth century a toll gate was placed across the road at the top of Highgate Hill and a monk collected a charge from passers-by. Nowadays the gate hangs high outside the Old Gate House tavern, it is thought to have been frequented by Dick Turpin, the notorious highwayman. The sound of the hoofs of a horse and the noise of jumping over a gate have been heard passing the house. When visiting the house he would make good his exit through a false cupboard whenever capture seemed imminent.. His ghost has been seen several times repeating the escapes. Here, too, came Widow Marnes, who while staying here was robbed and murdered. Her ghostly form has been seen appearing only when no children or animals are in the house. There is also record of a white-haired smuggler, murdered for his money, who has also been seen in various parts of the building.

Pond Square

To prove a theory Sir Francis Bacon killed a chicken and stuffed it with snow, thus taking part in a very early, sixteenth-century, experiment in the art of preserving food by freezing. Unfortunately, within a short time, Sir Francis took cold and died of pneumonia, and the hapless chicken has gone on flapping his ghostly wings to this day.

ISLINGTON

Old Queen's Head, Essex Road

(Nearest Underground station: Essex Road)

On one of her perambulations of the City of London and the surrounding area, it is said that Elizabeth I, visited the Earl of Essex in Islington, and stayed at his house in Essex Road. The house was built originally by Sir Walter Raleigh, and rebuilt in 1829 as the Old Queen's Head public house. It is haunted by the ghost of a woman said by some to be the Queen herself or someone who was associated with the building at some time in the past. There is also the story of plague victims being sealed in an upper room and it is their cries for mercy that are heard. A previous landlord had a nasty experience on a darkened staircase when some thing or person seemed to press against him. Whatever it was he never used the staircase in the dark again.

Collins Music Hall, Islington Green

(Nearest Underground station: Angel)

Until it was demolished in 1963 one of the most familiar buildings of Islington Green was Collins Music Hall whose now ghostly owner was last seen in 1960 walking through a wall in the cellar of the building. Deno Leno who in a moment of insanity committed suicide in 1904 who always played to full houses here and has also been seen wandering through the auditorium rehearsing his act before an empty theatre. He too has not been reported since the building was pulled down.

Tollington Park

(Nearest Underground station: Kentish Town)

In Tollington Park a landlord poisoned his tenant for a mere two hundred pounds, and although the house bombed in the Second World War has been completely rebuilt, unaccountable sounds are heard occasionally of a person choking to death.

Office Block, Holloway Road

(Nearest Underground station: Holloway Road)

On the site of the former Marlborough Theatre the Automobile Association built an office building to house their Computer Centre. The manager's office was situated on the site of one of the dressing rooms where an actor took his own life after getting badly heckled on the stage. Latterly he was seen moving about other parts of the building. When the Association left the place on moving to Basingstoke the ghost also disappeared!

39 Hilldrop Crescent

(Nearest Underground station: Kentish Town)

Doctor Crippen lived here for a few months in 1910 while working as a dentist in Oxford Street. Near the house was a small plot of wasteland where he would sit for hours in silent meditation. Some of the time he was plotting the murder of his wife, a not so successful music-hall artiste, and dreaming of her successor to be her replacement. The house was replaced by a block of flats after the last war. It was to the site of his house that his ghost has returned on a number of occasions and been seen by late-night revellers returning to their homes in the area.

LAMBETH

Imperial War Museum, Lambeth Road

(Nearest Underground station: Lambeth North)

It is not too difficult to reconstruct in one's mind the horrors of the former Bethlehem Hospital on the corner of Lambeth and St. George's Roads, now the Imperial War Museum. During the last war part of the building housed crews for the barrage balloons that were stationed in the nearby Harmondsworth Park. But, unfortunately some of the previous occupants had not left the premises and their shouting and screaming prevented the crews from having a quiet night's sleep. The eventual solution was to erect Nissan huts in the grounds and to leave the building to the ghosts. After the war when the building was restored to full museum use, no more was ever heard from the former occupants.

Lambeth Palace, Lambeth Road, Opposite Lambeth Bridge

(Nearest Underground station: Lambeth North)

Few ghosts can claim to have saved a life in more dramatic circumstances than at Lambeth Palace, the London home of the Archbishop of Canterbury. Here, during the Second World War, a man on fire-watching duty was prevented from entering a room by a door that had locked itself. Had he passed through the doorway he would certainly have been killed as the room received a direct hit from a high explosive bomb shortly afterwards.

Henry VIII's Queen, Anne Boleyn, lodged here during the early stages of her trial for adultery before being taken to the Tower of London and executed on Tower Green. It is not surprising that her ghost has been seen wandering through the rooms of the palace. She has also been seen on her spectral barge leaving the wharf of the palace on her way downstream.

The crypt of the palace has a strange atmosphere having been the depository for many years of human skulls and bones. These were discovered in various excavations, and one wonders what dark secrets some of them might tell.

It is in the Lollards Tower, so named after the Lollards who were followers of John Wycliffe, that the largest number of manifestations occur. Here the atmosphere is so strong that humans and animals alike have been prevented from walking up the stairs that lead to the room where prisoners were held awaiting trial. There is also a door in the tower that locks itself or swings freely of its own accord.

Finally there is Bishop Bonner, the persecutor and burner of heretics in the sixteenth century, whose bedroom on the north side of the courtyard is haunted by his figure. So fanatical a pursuer of Catholics that his plans included to burn or boil the Pope in a cauldron of molten lead.

STOCKWELL GREEN, OFF STOCKWELL ROAD

(Nearest Underground station: Stockwell)

In the latter half of the eighteenth century in one of the houses around Stockwell Green, then a quiet rural retreat, there lived a lady named Golding, with her one maid servant. A ghostly manifestation began on Twelfth Night (6th January) in 1722 when a number of plates and other pieces of crockery began falling down from the shelves in the kitchen for no apparent reason. When a friend of Mrs Golding's arrived and was invited to take a glass of wine with her, the bottle was broken by an unseen hand before the drink could be poured out from the bottle. While trying to escape from the falling pieces by running to a neighbour's house, some of her furniture, guided by the unseen hand, decided to follow her. Later, on Mrs Golding's death, the "dancing chairs" were sold for a high price.

VAUXHALL

(Nearest Underground station: Vauxhall)

Workmen on the Victoria Line, near Vauxhall, in 1968 believed that they were being watched by a ghost they named "The Quare Fellow". Had they disturbed a forgotten burial from yesteryear when the area was desolate and used for duelling?

SOUTHWARK

28 HORSELEY DOWN LANE, ANCHOR TAP PUBLIC HOUSE

(Nearest Underground station: London Bridge)

It is the ghost of "Charlie", so named by the locals, who performs the oddest of ghostly tricks here. He moves objects around the house moving them from one place to another — and sometimes back again!

CRUCIFIX LANE, HORNS PUBLIC HOUSE

(Nearest Underground station: London Bridge)

Before his death, in 1985, Canon John Pearce-Higgins would tell the story of how he performed the Rite of Exorcism at the Horns in Crucifix Lane. He had been invited by the tenants to clear the house of the ghosts that terrified the inhabitants by their appearances and actions. The ghosts were mother and child who once lived here but had been parted from each other. The child returned to look for her mother, both mother and child had died here. After the Canon's visit the child's spirit was rested but the mother continued to knock on walls and slam doors when walking through the rooms of the house.

ELEPHANT AND CASTLE (BR) STATION

(Nearest Underground station: Elephant and Castle)

Late in the evening footsteps are heard walking or running along the platform which, on investigation, by the staff is found to be empty

WALWORTH ROAD, THOMAS BECKET PUBLIC HOUSE

(Nearest Underground station: Elephant and Castle)

It cannot be pleasant to live on the site of one of the many former gallows located around the London area: the Thomas Becket public house in Walworth is no exception. An abundance of strange happenings have been reported such as cats and dogs refusing to enter certain upper rooms, bedroom doors locking themselves so securely that the local fire brigade has had to force them open. A glass was shattered into small pieces after a customer had scoffed at the idea of the existence of ghosts. Another sceptic waged a bet of five pounds that he would stay in one of the rooms — in broad daylight — for half an hour. Two minutes were enough for him and he quickly returned to the bar of the house and willingly paid over his five pounds.

Imperial War Museum

Tower of London

Bank of England

Tourist Information Offices London (Central)

BRITISH TRAVEL CENTRE
12 Regent Street,
Piccadilly,
London SW1Y 4PQ.
(personal callers only)

CITY OF LONDON INFORMATION CENTRE
St. Paul's Churchyard South,
London EC4.
Tel: 0171–935 2049

LIVERPOOL STREET
Liverpool Street Underground Station,
London EC2 7PN.

SOUTHWARK
Hay's Galleria,
Tooley Street,
London SE1 2HD
Tel: 0171–403 8299

SELFRIDGES
Basement Services Arcade,
Selfridges Store,
Oxford Street,
London W1.

VICTORIA
Victoria Station Forecourt,
London SW1V 1JU.

WATERLOO
London Visitor Centre,
Arrivals Hall,
Waterloo International Terminal,
London SE1 7LT.

Tourist Information
VISITORCALL — The phone guide to London

London Tourist Board operates a comprehensive range of recorded information services available twenty-four hours a day. Visitorcall is more than just a talking guidebook. It's updated daily to give you the latest information on London's events, exhibitions, theatres, concerts, places to visit, sightseeing, pageantry and much more.

Simply dial 0839 123 followed by the three numbers shown below for each subject.

WHAT'S ON

What's on this week	400
What's on — next three months	401
Sunday in London	407
Summer in the Parks	406
Christmas/Easter events	418
Changing the Guard	411

THEATRE

Popular West End shows	416
Beyond the West End	434
New productions/How to book	438

PLACES TO VISIT

Popular attractions	480
Museums	429
Palaces (including Buckingham Palace)	481
Greenwich/Military museums	482
Famous houses and gardens	483
Day trips from London	484

WHERE TO TAKE THE CHILDREN

What's on	404
Places to visit	424

OUT AND ABOUT

Getting around London	430
River trips/Boat hire	432
Guided tours/Walks	431
How to book a guide/ Bespoke guided tours	420
Getting to the airports	433
Shopping in London	486
Street markets	428
Pubs, restaurants and afternoon teas	485

ACCOMMODATION

General advice	435
Booking hotline	0171–824 8844

WEATHER

Met Office forecast for Greater London	0839 500 951

Calls charged at 39p per minute cheap rate, 49p per minute at all other times, plus any hotel/payphone surcharge (as at July 95). Please note that 0839 numbers are not accessible outside the UK.

Information for callers using push-button telephones 0171–971 0027. To order free cards listing all services call 0171–971 0026.

About the Author

John Wittich is an expert on the City of London and its environs, and has lectured and written on the subject for a number of years. Lecturing for the former Inner London Education Authority and its successors, the National Trust, Sutton College of Liberal Arts as well as freelance.

He also lectures at day and weekend courses on Architecture at various adult colleges. During the past three summers he has conducted courses at Millfield Village of Education, Millfield School, Somerset, as well as the Sutton College of Liberal Arts.

A Guide-lecturer, qualified by the London Tourist Board and Convention Bureau, he has journeyed all over the countryside in search of places of architectural and historical interest. He is a Fellow of both the Royal Society of Arts and the Ancient Monuments Society, and a Life Member of the Royal Photographic Society.

Freeman of the City of London, Parish Clerk of the Parish of St. Mary Aldermanbury in the City of London, Master (1995–96) of the Worshipful Company of Parish Clerks of the City of London, and a Liveryman of the Worshipful Company of Woolmen of the City of London.

Between 1960 and 1987, with his then partner Ron Phillips, he founded and ran Off-Beat Tours of London, the organisation that pioneered walking tours in and around the City of London. Since 1987 he has run his own walking-tours operations — J.W. Travel — which now forms part of J.W. Promotions. He still offers members of the public that special service of showing them the "sights behind the sights". In 1994 he founded the ITS (the In Touch Society) as a means of keeping in touch with his students and friends who like to "wander through the city on foot in search of history and the unusual". He can also offer a lecture service.

PUBLICATIONS

Discovering London Curiosities – London Villages –London Street Names – London's Inns and Taverns – London's Parks and Squares – Catholic London – Churches Cathedrals and Chapels – History and Guide to the Parish of St. John the Evangelist, Hyde Park Crescent, London W2 – A Guide to Bayswater – Exploring Cathedrals – The Hidden Treasures of Regent's Park – History and Guide to the Parish of St. Magnus the Martyr, Lower Thames Street, London EC2 – Curiosities of Surrey – Off–Beat Walks in London – Fun-fax Spot it Guide to London – Exploring London.

Index

Duke of York's Theatre, St. Martin's Lane (see page 64).

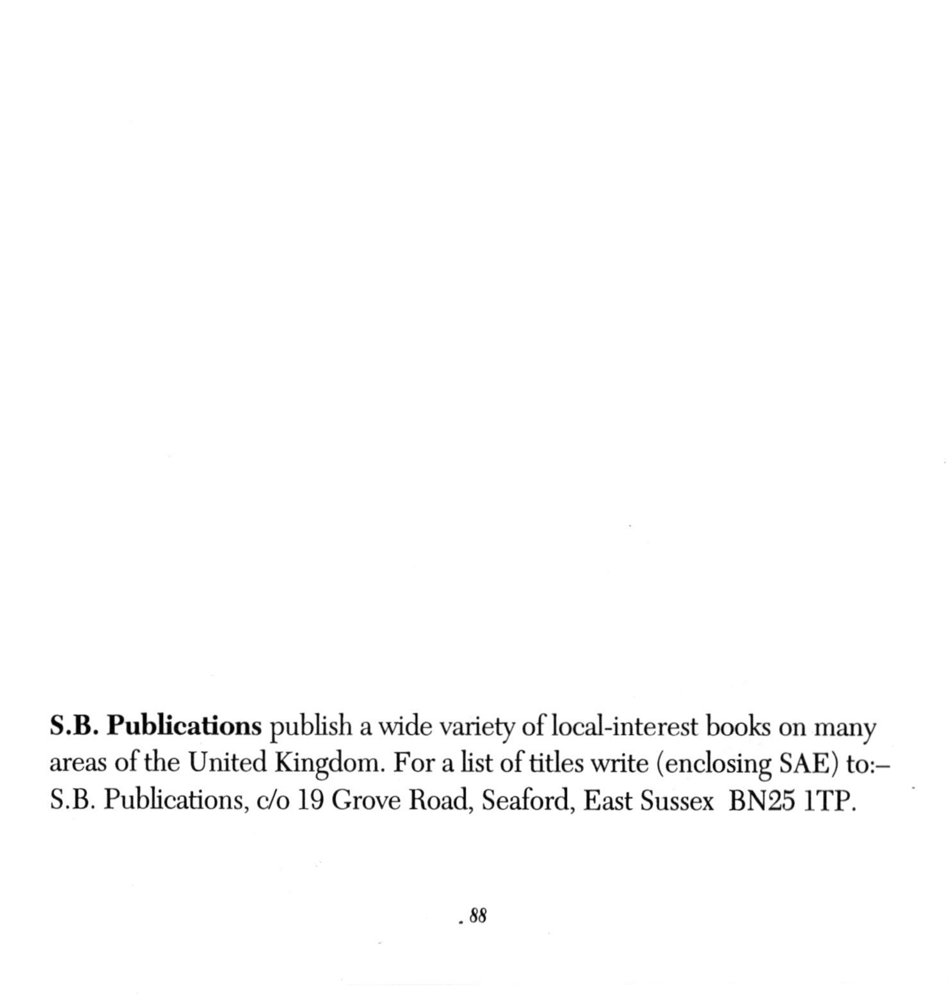